Helion & Company Limited
26 Willow Road
Solihull
West Midlands
B91 1UE
England
Tel. 0121 705 3393
Fax 0121 711 4075
email: info@helion.co.uk
website: www.helion.co.uk
Twitter: @helionbooks
Visit our blog http://blog.helion.co.uk

Published by Helion & Company 2017
Designed and typeset by Farr out Publications, Wokingham, Berkshire
Cover designed by Paul Hewitt, Battlefield Design (www.battlefield-design.co.uk)
Printed by Henry Ling Limited, Dorchester, Dorset

ISBN 978-1-911512-58-5

British Library Cataloguing-in-Publication Data
A catalogue record for this book is available from the British Library

CONTENTS

PART 1: THE ROUTE TO WAR

1
BRAZILIAN MILITARY AVIATION UNTIL 1941

The Brazilian Military Aviation had a slow start, initially with the creation of the *Escola Brasileira de Aviação*, formed in 1912 and expanded at Campo dos Afonsos, near Rio de Janeiro, on 2 February 1914. The school was a private one, but received a contract from the War Ministry to train pilots for the Army and Navy, with three Farman, five Bleriot and one Aerotorpedo planes, all purchased in Europe by the owners of the school, who were all Italian. However, lack of payment by the government and the beginning of the First World War led to the rescinding of the contract by the Italians on 18 July, by which time 11 officers of the Army and six of the Navy were trained.

After this experience, the Navy took two years to create their own Naval Aviation School, while the Army only followed suit in 1919, when the end of the war in Europe made possible the easy purchase of new and more modern flight equipment.

The first military use of an airplane in Brazil occurred in 1914 when Lieutenant Ricardo Kirk, who obtained his flight brevet in France in 1912, commanded a small team that made reconnaissance flights during a campaign against insurgency groups in the area of Contestado, to the north of Santa Catarina State. Initially, a Morane Saulnier and a Bleriot were sent to the area, but they were destroyed when the train that was carrying them caught fire. After this, by the end of the year three Morane Saulniers were sent; with one of these, on 4 January 1915, the first experimental reconnaissance flight was made from the *Campo de Aviação de União da Vitória* (Victory Union Airfield), in the city of Porto União, operations ending on 1 March with the death of Lieutenant Kirk in an accident.

The Brazilian Naval Aviation

On 23 August 1916, by decree 12167, the *Escola da Aviaçao Naval de la Marinha do Brasil* (Brazilian Navy Naval Aviation School) was inaugurated at Isla de las Enxadas in Rio de Janeiro. The first planes were three Curtiss F flying boats, which were followed in 1918 by fifteen new planes, including four Curtiss Fs, six Curtiss HS-2Ls, two FBA Mark Bs, two Standard JHs and one *Borel*. In 1919, two Farman F-41s, nine Curtiss N-9Hs, two Ansaldo ISVAs, five Macchi M-9s and three Macchi M-7s were added. Until then, all were seaplanes and were mainly used for training and reconnaissance, while the HS-2Ls had the capacity to carry two 104kg bombs, being the first armed planes in Brazil.

In 1920, five Avro 504Ks were purchased, being the first landplanes, arriving together with four Aeromarine 40s and 10 Curtiss MFs, followed in 1921 by two Farman F-51s. In 1923, the *Centro de Aviación Naval* (Naval Aviation Centre) of Rio de Janeiro was created at Ponta do Galeão, on another island at Guanabara Bay, to where the *Escola da Aviação Naval* was moved. In the same year, most of the initial seaplanes acquired were retired, replaced by 14 Curtiss F-5Ls for maritime surveillance and bombing, 12 Sopwith 7F-1 Snipe fighters, 12 Avro 504Ks and 18 Ansaldo SVA-10s for observation. By that time, bases had been created at Florianópolis and Santos, besides that at Rio de Janeiro.

During the Internal Revolution of 1924, the Naval Aviation participated very actively, performing patrol, observation and attack missions. After these events, there was a crucial lack of budget until 1927, restricting operations and impeding new acquisitions, apart from four Curtiss JN-4D Jennys in 1925. In 1927, three Consolidated NY-2s arrived, followed in 1928 by six Avro 504N/Os and one Consolidated PT-3.

In 1930 another revolution took place, which resulted in the presidency of Getulio Vargas, under whom a new era began. In 1931, 11 Savoia-Marchetti SM-55As were added, together with three Martin PMs and six Vought O2U-2A Corsairs, to create a reconnaissance unit, while the Naval Aviation School had four Avro 504N/Os, the Consolidated NY-2s and the PT-3. On 3 October 1931, the *Corpo Aviaçao* (Aviation Corps) was created, and with it the aviation cadre for officers and petty officers.

By 1932, 12 de Havilland DH-60T Moth Trainers and six Boeing 256 fighters were received, followed in 1933 by eight Waco CSOs, five DH-83 Fox Moths (which were the first planes with transport capacity), 20 Fairey Gordons, 12 extra Moth Trainers, eight Vought V-66B Corsairs and 17 DH-82 and DH-82A Tiger Moths. Due to the war between Bolivia and Paraguay, the Naval Aviation was deployed to the border with those two countries, to be sure they didn't violate the frontier. For that, the *4º Divisão de Reconhecimento y Bombardeio* (4th Reconnaissance and Bombing Division) was created, based at Alto Solimoes, with three Gordons. At that time, the Naval Aviation

Fairey Gordon of the Brazilian Naval Aviation.

Boeing 267 of the Brazilian Army, one of the first real fighters used by the force.

Vought V-65B Corsair of the Brazilian Army, used for attack and reconnaissance.

Fairey Gordon used by the Naval Aviation.

The Navy operated the Boeing 256 as their main fighter before the Second World War.

Martin PM of the Naval Aviation, used for maritime patrols.

One of the three Liore et Olivier 25 Bn4s, the first heavy bombers of the Army Aviation.

One of the five Macchi M-9s of the Naval Aviation.

took part in many exercises of the fleet, and also had bases at Ladário, Santa Catarina and Río Grande do Sul.

Also in 1933 the first air demonstration squadron in Brazil was created, with Boeing 256s, which made their first aerobatic demonstration during the inauguration of the Base Aeronaval Nº1 of Uruguayan Naval Aviation at Isla Libertad in Montevideo.

One year later, the *Correo Aéreo Naval* (Naval Air Mail) was created to improve the communications of the force, using the Fox Moth, but in 1935 four Waco CJCs and 10 Waco CPF F-5s were added. In 1936, a contract was signed with Focke Wulf Flugzeug Baer GMBH of Germany, for the construction under license of 40 FW-44J *Stieglitz*, 30 FW-56 *Stösser*, 45 FW-58 *Weihe* and some FW-200 Condor, but production of the *Stösser* and the Condor was cancelled when the Second World War began. In total, the Navy received 41 Fw-44s and 14 Fw-58s, while 17 additional *Weihe* were delivered directly to the *Força Aérea Brasileira*.

The last acquisitions before 1941 were one de Havilland DH-84 Dragon Rapide, one Luscombe Phantom and 12 North American NA-46s in 1939, followed in 1940 by four Beechcraft D17As and one Stinson 105.

The Army Aviation

In 1918, the *Exército Brasileiro* (Brazilian Army) began preparations to organise their own flight school at Campo dos Afonsos, contracting French instructors and mechanics.This was officially inaugurated on 10 July 1919, equipped with *Aribú* and *Alagōas* planes (built in Brazil), besides a Morane Saulnier M.S.21, six Nieuport 24 Bis E1s, 14 Nieuport 83E2s, seven Nieuport 82E2s and three Sopwith 1A2s, the latter used with weapons on reconnaissance and bombing missions. In the following year, 30 Breguet 14 A2/B2s were purchased for bombing and reconnaissance, together with 20 Spad 7C1 and one S.E.5A fighters, 20 Nieuport 21E1s for training and a single Caproni Ca-45 for bombing, being the first twin-engined plane of the force. They were followed by two Caudron G.4s and 28 Nieuport 80Es in 1921.

The first enlargment of the deployment of the Military Aviation occurred on 5 July 1922, when the *Grupo de Aviação no Sul* (Aviation

One of the locally built Focke Wulf Fw-44Js used by the Navy.

One of the Waco CSOs which were purchased by the Army and later transferred to the FAB.

Focke Wulf Fw-58B *Weihe*. They were the main bombers of the Navy until they were transferred to the Air Force.

The Breguet 14A2 called São Borja.

Waco CJC of the Army Aviation.

Boeing 256 of the Navy.

Group in the South) was created at Santa María, composed of the *1° Esquadrilha de Bombardeio* (1st Bombing Squadron) with four Breguet 14s, the *1° Esquadrilha de Caça* (1st Fighter Squadron) with nine Spad 17s and the support of the *3° Companhia Provisória de Parque de Aviação* (3rd Aviation Workshop Provisory Company). Also, the 3° *Esquadrilha se Observação* (3rd Observation Squadron) was based at the town of Alegrete with six Breguet 14s. By then it was considered that the main threat on the borders was Argentina, especially because the area of industrial development in Brazil was to the south, close to the frontier with that country.

Between 19 and 28 July 1924, the *Esquadrilha de Aperfeiçoamento* (Improvement Squadron) of the *Escola de Aviação Militar* was deployed to São Paulo State to fight a revolutionary movement, performing 21 bombing, reconnaissance and liaison missions with six Breguet 14s, two Nieuport 15s and two Spad Herbemont (from eight received that year), operating from Mogi das Cruzes. Later, between 18 August and 26 September, the planes were again deployed to fight the revolutionaries, leaving the city of São Paulo and moving to the interior of the state, finishing with a third deployment between October of that year and March 1925.

The revolutionary movements slowed considerably the development of the Military Aviation, mainly because of suspicion about the loyalty of pilots.

The *Arma Aviação do Exército* (Army Aviation Arm), created in 1927, was a big step forward, as it became on equal terms with the other armed forces and meant recognition of its importance to the Army. The Military Aviation School started to depend on the Army Aviation Arm, the former being the only unit until then, with all the fighter, bomber and reconnaissance aircraft. The next year, six Breguet

Line up at Campo dos Afonsos, during the visit of a formation of B-17Bs of the USAAF in 1938.

Nieuport 24 Bis E1 of the Brazilian Army Aviation.

Caudron G.4 used by the Army for aerial photography.

XIX A2B2s, three Caudron 59s, 10 Morane Saulnier MS-35Ep2s and six Potez 25A2s arrived, followed in 1929 by seven flying boat Schreck FBA-17 HMT-2s, which were the first planes of this kind for the Army Aviation. Many other planes were also introduced that year, including 15 Morane Saulnier MS-130ET2s, eight Potez 33s for transport and light bombing, five Wibault 73C1 fighters and one Caudron 140 for reconnaissance and bombing. On 20 January 1929, the order was given to put serials on planes according to their mission, with 'K' for planes of the *Escola da Aviação* and 'A' to 'J' for the units still to be created, then using numbers from 110 to 199 for fighters, and from 210 onwards for trainers.

The first unit outside the *Escola de Aviação* was the *Grupo Misto de Aviação* (Joint Aviation Group), created in 1931, based at Campo dos Afonsos and equipped with 10 Potez 25s (from 18 that arrived in 1930), together with some Curtiss Fledglings, from a total of 14 introduced that year. By 1930, the fleet was also increased with 18

Morane Saulnier MS-130 ET2 in use by the Brazilian Army.

Morane Saulnier MS-147 EP2 of the Army.

Potez 25 TOE used by the Brazilian Army.

Morane Saulnier MS-147 EP2s, one MS-149 EP2 and one Breguet XIXA GR, while in 1931 new planes included four Amiot 122 Bp3s, two Farman F-74s, four Nieuport Delage 72C1s and three Lioré et Olivier 25Bn4 twin-engined bombers.

Meanwhile, in 1932, seven Curtiss O-1E Falcon attack planes, 15 de Havilland DH-60T Moth Trainers, one Fleet 7, 37 Vought V-65B Corsairs, 20 Waco RNFs, 41 Waco CSOs, eight Boeing 256s and nine Boeing 267 fighters. During the next year they were followed by 12 Fleet 10D, 12 Bellanca CH-300 Special Pacemakers, 22 Waco CTOs and by 25 Waco CHCs. Acquisitions continued with 15 Curtiss CW-16s, 30 Waco CPF F-5s and one Waco UMF-3 in 1935.

During 1932, the Army Aviation again entered into action during a new revolutionary attempt, this time against President Getúlio

Breguet XIX A GR used for long distance flights in the Thirties.

The Vultee V-11 were the first all-metal attack planes of the Brazilian Army. They were still in use by the Second World War and one made an attack on a submarine.

The sole example of the Vultee V-11 fitted with floats was offered to the Brazilian Naval Aviation. It was re-fitted with wheels and acquired by the Army.

One of the Fw-58 *Weihes* in use by the Brazilian Naval Aviation until they were transferred to the Air Force in 1941.

Vargas, who had assumed power in 1930. The *Grupo Misto de Aviação* operated against the troops of São Paulo State.

Deployment of the Army Aviation began in 1933, with the creation of the *1º Regimento* at Campo dos Afonsos (using as a basis the *Grupo Misto de Aviação*), the *3º Regimento* at Canoas (Porto Alegre) and the *5º Regimento* at Curitiba, from the basis of a detachment created during the revolution of 1932, equipped with seven Vought Corsairs. They were followed in 1934 by the *2º Regimento* at Campo de Marte in São Paulo, from the basis of the *Destacamento de Aviação de São Paulo*, with three Vought Corsairs, the *Destacamento de Aviação de Campo Grande* and the *7º Regimento* at Belém in 1936. In 1934, the *Destacamento de Belo Horizonte* was created, which was the basis for the later creation of the *4º Regimento*. The same happened with the *Destacamento de Fortaleza*, created in that year and which in 1936 became the *6º Regimento*.

Last purchases before the war

By the mid-Thirties, the aircraft of the Army Aviation were very old, as the force was mainly equipped with biplanes - fighters and bombers, trainers and reconnaissance planes, with very few light transports, mainly used by the *Correo Aéreo Nacional* (National Air Mail). Because of this, after 1935 and thanks to the experience acquired in the different revolutionary conflicts, adding to what they saw in the region and around the world, the fleet began to be modernised, giving the force a respectable power for the region. The following were the last acquisitions until 1941.

For elementary training they bought 16 Avro 626 Trainers, 11 locally built Muniz M-7s and 20 Muniz M-9s, while for basic training there were 30 Stearman A-76C3s, 20 Stearman A75L3s and they received two Focke Wulf Fw-44Js donated by the FMA factory in Argentina, who built them under license. For advanced training they obtained 30 North American NA-72s, the first examples of the Texan family, which would become widely known in Brazil. By that time, the first medium transports were also acquired, with eight Lockheed 12As, while they also received two Consolidated Commodores which had belonged to *Panair do Brasil*, which were used in the Amazon region. For liaison they purchased 37 Waco EGC-7s and two Bellanca Skyrockets, while for attack sorties the force acquired 25 Vultee V11GB-2s and a single V-11GB-2F with floats (later transformed with wheeled landing gear), which were the most powerful planes of the force until 1941.

On 27 November 1939 it was determined that the *2º*, *4º*, *6º* and *7º Regimento* would become the *Corpos de Base Aérea* (Air Base Corps), while the 8º *Corpo de Base Aérea* was created at Campo Grande, where there was the *III Grupo* of the 2º *Regimento*. The *Corpos 1, 3* and *5* gathered the air units of the 1º, 3º and 5º *Regimento* respectively, which kept functioning.

After the invasion of Poland by Germany in September 1939, which instigated the Second World War, and the beginning of operations by German submarines in the Atlantic Ocean in December that year, some V-65 Corsairs were deployed to Recife and Belém to patrol the seas and detect the possible presence of submarines in Brazilian waters, despite the planes not being the most suitable for such missions. Anyhow, the first German and Italian submarines only started operations in the region in 1942.

2
THE FORÇA AÉREA BRASILEIRA

Following the tendency of some of the pioneer countries in aviation, such as the United Kingdom, Italy and France, which separated their air forces from dependency on the Army, on 20 January 1941, president Getúlio Vargas signed Decree Nº 2,961 which determined the creation of the *Ministério da Aeronáutica* (Ministry of Aeronautics). Article 5 of the decree stated that "the institutions, dependencies, organizations and services of the national aviation activity, currently subordinated to the Ministry of War, Navy and Public Works, will be under the jurisdiction of the Ministry of Aeronautics". Article 8 added that "all the military personnel of the Aeronautic Arm of the Army and the Naval Aviation Corps, including the reserves, will become a unique corporation subordinated to the Ministry of Aeronautics, with the name *Forças Aéreas Nacionais*". This name was changed on 22 May, by Decree Nº 3,302, for the name *Força Aérea Brasileira* (FAB, Brazilian Air Force). Doctor Joaquim Pedro Salgado Filho was appointed as minister and was in charge of its organization, with one of his assistants being Captain Aviator Nero Moura.

Weihes of the Naval Aviation at Galeão Naval Air Base.

One of the three SM-79Ts received by the Army in 1938. They were transferred to the FAB in 1941 where they served until 1943. In the picture it still has Italian colours; later they received the Brazilian flag on the tail and the serials were removed.

The *Força Aérea Brasileira* was organised with the following regiments:

- 1º *Regimento de Aviação*, at Río de Janeiro (with bases at Campo dos Afonsos received from the Army and at Galeão from the Naval Aviation), inherited from the Navy the 1º *Flotilha de Aviões de Esclarecimento e Bombardeio* (1st Bombing and Surveillance Airplane Fleet), 1º *Flotilha de Aviões de Observação* (1st Observation Airplane Fleet), 1º *Flotilha de Aviões de Bombardeio e Patrulha* (1st Bombing and Patrol Airplane Fleet) and 1º and 2º *Esquadrilha de Adestramento Militar* (1st and 2nd Military Training Squadrons). From the Army, the FAB kept the units that were already part of the regiment:
- 2º *Corpo de Base Aérea*, at Campo de Marte, São Paulo.
- 3º *Regimento de Aviação*, at Canoas
- 4º *Corpo de Base Aérea*, at Belo Horizonte
- 5º *Regimento de Aviação*, at Curitiba
- 6º *Corpo de Base Aérea*, at Fortaleza
- 7º *Corpo de Base Aérea*, at Belém
- 8º *Corpo de Base Aérea*, at Campo Grande.

The country was divided into three Military Air Zones, the first covering the entire north of the country and the coast down to Rio de Janeiro, the second covering the centre of the country to São Paulo state and the third covering the entire south.

Later, on 25 October 1941, the country was divided into five zones, the first in the north and west, the second in the north-east, the third

Personnel of the Argentine and Paraguayan Armies visiting a FAB base in September 1941.

A Boeing 267 transferred to the FAB.

Some of the first Texans of the FAB.

A Brazilian SM-79T shortly after arriving in the country, still with Italian markings.

A rare picture of a FAB Boeing 267.

in the central coastal region of the country, the fourth in the south and the last one in Matto Grosso State, which later also included São Paulo State.

The FAB's equipment by that time was similar to other air forces in the region, which quickly became obsolete with the progress in aviation of the countries at war. The Navy transferred the following

One of the Curtiss P-36s used by the FAB.

A Vultee V-11 of the FAB.

aircraft to the FAB: three Beechcraft D-17As, two Boeing 256s, one de Havilland DH-60T, 10 de Havilland DH-82 and DH-82As, two de Havilland DH-83s, 14 Focke Wulf Fw-58B *Weihe*, thirty-six Focke Wulf Fw-44J *Stieglitz*, one Luscombe Phantom, 12 North American NA-46s, one Stinson 105, one Vought V-66B, three Waco CSOs, four Waco CPF F-5s and three Waco CJCs.

The Army transferred 16 Avro 626s, 12 Bellanca Pacemakers, two Bellanca Skyrockets, three Savoia Marchetti S-79Ts, five Boeing 256s, seven Boeing 267s, two Consolidated Commodores, six Curtiss Falcons, one Curtiss Fledgling, one Fleet 7, eight Fleet 10s, two Focke Wulf Fw-44Js, eight Lockheed L.12As, seven Muniz M-7s, 16 Muniz M-9s, 30 North American NA-72s, 27 Stearman A76C3 and B76C3s, 20 Stearman A75L3s, 29 Vought V-65Bs, 24 Vultee V-11GB2s, 25 Waco CSOs, 27 Waco CPF F-5s, 23 Waco CJCs, 29 Waco EGC-7s and one Waco UMF.

The main combat planes were the five Boeing 256 (F4B) and seven Boeing 267s as fighters, 29 Vought V.65 Corsairs for observation and attack, 14 Focke Wulf Fw-58 *Weihe* and three Savoia S-79s as bombers, and 24 Vultee V.11GB-2s for attack and reconnaissance, but all were old and only in a small quantity for a country the size of Brazil.

In total, they were 97 planes from the Navy and 331 from the Army, but during 1941 the DH-60T, DH-83, Curtiss Falcon and Fledgling were retired. These were followed in 1942 by the DH-82, Luscombe Phantom, Vought V-66B, Stinson 105, Consolidated Commodore and Muniz M-7, while the others were mostly used for training.

By that time, the fleet was not only small and old compared to the major world powers, but also with its main competitor in the region, Argentina, which had a fleet, between the Army Aviation and Navy, consisting of Curtiss Hawk 75-O fighters, Northrop 8A attack planes, Martin 139WAN and WAA, Fw-58 *Weihe* and Junkers K-43 bombers, Junkers W-34, Ju-52, FMA Ae.M.B.2 Bombi, Lockheed 10 and 12 as transports, Vought V-65F and V-142 for observation, and Consolidated P2Y-31 for maritime surveillance, besides many other transport and training aircraft.

It was clear that a modernization of Brazilian air power was urgently needed, because the country had not made any important

One of the NA-44s of the FAB.

purchases of modern aircraft before the war, something that was done by Argentina. Also, the global war was approaching the coasts of America, and Brazil was an important place, because of its proximity to Africa, besides having many natural resources that the country could provide to those nations involved in the war.

The first step to be taken was to modernise the training fleet, which only had as efficient aircraft the Fw-44J, Stearmans and NA-46 and 72, but they were not enough to cope with the expansion plans developed by the air force, especially from 1942 when the country entered the war.

In the meantime, the expansion of air bases and civil airports along the coastline was ordered in July 1941 to prepare them for the operation of bigger planes that were expected to be acquired in the future. Works began on the runways at Amapá, Belém, São Luiz, Fortaleza, Natal, Recife, Maceió and Salvador, while new facilities and buildings started to be built at Belém, Fortaleza, Natal, Recife and Salvador, to house the new air units. Most of the works would be done in co-operation with the US government, which contracted Pan American Airport Corporation (a subsidiary of the Pan American airline, which operated all across Latin America) to negotiate the construction or expansion of the many aerodromes in the region to be used as air bases in case the United States entered the war. Among those airports were the one at Natal, and the Brazilian government authorised this plan on 25 July 1941, with the works to be carried out by *Panair do Brasil*, another subsidiary of Pan American.

3

BRAZIL IN THE SECOND WORLD WAR

As soon as the Second World War began, the Brazilian government decided to stay neutral, with the aim of not being affected by the conflict, despite many sectors of the country's society being in favour of supporting one side or the other, mainly the Allies. Nevertheless, the government of Getulio Vargas tried to keep its neutrality, despite the major interest in the country by the Allied and Axis powers, Brazil being a bridgehead between Africa (and hence Europe) and America, and also an important source of natural resources.

US operations in Brazil

In August 1941, the United States began, with Brazilian authorization, to transport, via Brazil and Africa, planes for use by British forces. The US government had been worried since the beginning of the war about the lack of defences along the Brazilian coast, especially in the area closest to Africa, as this was considered the place where any attempted invasion of America by European forces could take place. This worry increased after the fall of France in 1940, as the French colonies in Western Africa could be used for such a purpose by the victorious Germans. This was one of the main concerns of the Americans, who did not want the war to be extended into the Americas. The intention of the US government to send troops to protect these coasts was not well received in Brazil, as politicians feared an intervention by the United States, but they were allowed to perform some discrete maritime patrol operations on the north-east Brazilian coast and to construct aerodromes to transport the planes to Africa, as detailed in the previous chapter. The Brazilian government proposed that the US finance the re-equipping of the Brazilian Armed Forces, so they could defend themselves.

When the United States entered the war after the Japanese attack on Pearl Harbor on 7 December 1941, they started to put pressure on the Latin American nations to break relations with the Axis countries, which Brazil abided by on 28 January 1942.

In the meantime, as war was approaching the American coasts and before the attack on Pearl Harbor, in July 1941 the US Navy organised their Atlantic patrol forces into Patrol Wings 3, 5, 7, 8 and 9, each with four squadrons, and divided the area into five 'Sea Frontiers', on the east coast, Canadian coast, Gulf of Mexico, Panama and the Caribbean, followed later by ones in Bermuda, Açores, Brasil, Freetown (Sierra

One of the three B-18 Bolos received by the FAB.

Italian submarine *Archimede* which operated in Brazilian waters.

The Italian submarine *Calvi* was one of the first to operate near the Brazilian coast.

The freighter *Arará* which was sunk by *U-507*.

Leone), Atlantic south-west and Atlantic south-east.

Each frontier started to receive airplanes and ships to protect their own merchant ships, and the entrance of the United States into the war found them in the middle of carrying this out. Despite it initially being planned to protect the neutrality of the American states, maritime patrol operations began on 11 December 1941 along the north coast of Brazil, from Recife, Natal and Salvador, with ships and four Consolidated PBY-5 Catalinas of VP-52 Squadron, of Patrol Wing 3 of the US Navy, under command of Lieutenant Commander Thomas A. Turner, whose base was in Panama. They were deployed with the support of the tenders USS *Greene* and *Thrush*.

The freighter *Baependi* which was sunk by *U-507* on 15 August 1942.

A B-24 Liberator of Squadron VB-107 of the US Navy flying near the coast of Natal.

Brazilian ships sunk

Meanwhile, the war was approaching Brazil, with submarines attacking three ships of foreign flags relatively close to the Brazilian coast, but more than 400km off them. As soon as war with the United States began in December 1941, the Germans sent six U-Boats to the American coast under Operation *Paukenschlag*, and in the first three months of 1942 they sank 60 ships.

The consequences of Brazil's rupture of relations with the Axis countries were immediate, as German and Italian submarines began torpedoing Brazilian ships on 14 February, starting with the *Cabedello* merchant ship off the coast of the United States, sunk by the Italian submarine *Da Vinci*. This was followed on the next day by the *Buarque*, close to Norfolk, Virginia, and on 18 February by the *Olinda*, near Saint Lucia, both sunk by the German submarine *U-432*. On 7 March, the *U-155* sank the *Arabutã*, and on the following day the *U-94* sank the *Cairu*, followed on May 1 by the *Parnaíba*. The attacks continued, and by August a total of 22 ships had been attacked, most of them sunk, and with a high death toll.

All of these attacks were made near the coast of the United States or in the Caribbean. Close to the American coast, inside the so-called Panamerican Security Zone, established at a time of neutrality for all countries on the continent, the ships sailed alone, without convoys being organised. The lack of protection of merchant ships in the Caribbean and Gulf of Mexico, together with the intensity of traffic, led to the launch of operations by U-Boats in the region, first in the Gulf and then – with Operation *Neuland* – in the Caribbean, mainly close to the coasts of Venezuela and Trinidad, where there were many ships carrying oil from Venezuela and the refineries in Aruba and Curaçao, and bauxite from British Guiana. Between February and June 1942, 114 ships were sunk in this area.

Up until this point, the only operations of U-Boats in the South Atlantic took place close to the African coast, with six ships sunk by *U-65* in 1940 and 47 in 1941 by *U-69*, *U-105* and *U-124*, one of them close to the Brazilian coast.

A PBM-3S Mariner of the US Navy; the same model was used off the coasts of Brazil.

The Italian submarine *Alpino Bagnolini* which operated in Brazilian waters.

The submarine *U-662* during the attack by a Catalina of Squadron VP-94 of the US Navy. The attack, on 21 July 1943, ended with the sinking of the submarine.

As the Axis powers saw an opportunity to damage the supplies of the Allies in that area, the Italian submarine *Calvi* left Bordeaux on 7 March, heading for the Brazilian coast, starting by exploring the coast off Maranhão State, near the cities of São Luis, Fortaleza and Natal. On 1 April, the *Calvi* made its first attack, against the US-flagged tanker *T.C. McCobb*. Later, after attempting unsuccessfully to attack other ships, on 9 April the Italians sank the Norwegian merchant ship *Balkis*, and on the 12th the Panamanian tanker *Bean Brush*, before returning then to base. This patrol by the Italian submarine verified to both the Italians and Germans that there were almost no enemy forces in the zone, while there was an important traffic of merchant ships. They therefore decided to deploy four Italian submarines, the *Barbarigo*, *Alpino Bagnolini*, *Cappellini* and *Archimede*, the first on 17 May and the others on the 23rd.

Due to these moves, which had been expected by the Americans, the US Navy created Patrol Wing 11 on San Juan, Puerto Rico, and Patrol Wing 12 at Key West, Florida, also starting to operate from Trinidad and later from other Caribbean bases. On 7 April 1942, the US Navy deployed their VP-83 Squadron of Patrol Wing 5 to Natal (under command of Patrol Wing 11), led by Lieutenant Commander Ralph Sperry Clarke, replacing the detachment of VP-52, and started patrol missions over the coast of northern Brazil, employing six PBY-5 Catalina flying boats. As the Catalinas were also equipped with landing gear, they started operations at Parnamirim airfield, Natal's air base, while the planes of VP-52 flew from the Potengy River. They started operations four days later, and on 13 July were joined by six extra planes, one of them performing an attack against a submarine while en route between Trinidad and the British Guiana. Unfortunately, while arriving at Natal, one of the planes crashed and four of the seven crew members were killed, the others being rescued by a fishing vessel after being found the next day by one of the Catalinas.

Operation conditions in Natal were hard, as the base still lacked many facilities and the airfields to where they deployed on their missions often had no facilities at all.

Meanwhile, as some intelligence reports suggested the possible occupation of Fernando de Noronha Island, 350km off Brazil's north-east coast by the Germans to create a base for their submarines, a detachment of the Army was sent to the island on 15 April.

Those fears were reinforced when, on 18 May, the Italian submarine *Barbarigo* attacked the merchant ship *Comandante Lyra* close to the island, launching a torpedo and then opening fire with its gun. The crew managed to send an SOS and then abandoned ship. The ships of the US Navy's Task Force 23.2, which was operating in the area, went to the ship's aid, together with some of Task Force 23.3, finding her on the following day. The castaways were rescued and the ship was recovered by the USS *Thrush* seaplane tender, with the support of the Brazilian tug *Heitor Perdigão*, protectied by the Catalinas of VP-83 and the cruisers USS *Milwaukee* and *Cincinnati*. That was the first Brazilian ship attacked close to the coast of Brazil, proving it was vital to increase the presence of patrol aircraft all over the coast, especially from Santos harbour, near São Paulo, to the north.

On 20 May, the *Barbarigo* attacked the USS *Milwaukee*, which was sailing next to the destroyer USS *Moffer*, but missed the target.

Active participation

On 22 August 1942, Brazil announced they were at war with the Axis countries and on 12 September their naval forces were put under operational command of Task Force 3 of the US Navy, under command of Vice-Admiral Jonas Ingram. They formed the South Atlantic Force, with responsibility over the seas from Trinidad & Tobago to the south of Buenos Aires province in Argentina, reaching the middle of the ocean, with the eastern part left for operations based in Africa. Initially, operations would be fully controlled by the US forces, but this wasn't accepted by the Brazilian Air Force, and Brigadeiro-do-ar Eduardo Gomes, commander of the 1st and 2nd Zona Aérea, worked with Ingram and divided the forces into Orange and Blue groups. The first would include US forces for long-range missions over the maritime routes, while the second would be Brazilian planes based in the north-east of the country and patrolling the coast from Fortaleza y Maceió. The attacks would be conducted as soon as a submarine was detected, and command of the operation would be in the hands of the most highly ranked officer in place.

On 29 January 1943, during a meeting at Natal between Getulio Vargas and US president Franklin D. Roosevelt, it was decided that Brazil would actively participate in the war, first sending an expeditionary force of the Army to Europe, followed by a force of the FAB. The problem was that the FAB had only just started having some flight experience with the P-40, and the planes that were then being used in Europe were even more advanced. Nevertheless, it was decided to send a fighter group and an observation squadron to the Mediterranean theatre of operatioms, and on 7 December 1943 a team of Brazilian Army and Air Force officers departed on a Consolidated C-87 Liberator to Algeria, to observe the operations of the Allies in the area and study all that would be necessary for the Brazilians to operate there. These units, like those already operating along the Brazilian coast, would be subordinated to US forces.

PART 2: OPERATIONS ON THE BRAZILIAN COAST

4
RE-EQUIPPING AND FIRST ANTI-SUBMARINE OPERATIONS

Before the ending of relations with the Axis countries and the entry of the United States into the war, but considering the strategic importance of Brazil and the need to modernise its aviation - which was practically obsolete - the country benefited from the signing of a Lend-Lease agreement on 3 March 1942. From this time the FAB began to be re-equipped with modern US materiel.

The first requirement of the air force was training aircraft, not only because those in service were old, but because they were very few and the need to train new pilots was huge. Different types were therefore acquired from the United States, mainly Vultee BT-15s, AT-6 Texans and Fairchild PT-19s, which started to arrive between April and June 1942, when a total of 50 BT-15s and 10 Beechcraft C-18Ss made the ferry flight from the United States, the latter to train pilots on twin-engined planes and also for liaison. Between July and August, 30 Fairchild PT-19s flew in, followed by another 10 between October and November.

To increase the transport capacity, 10 Lockheed Lodestars were purchased, the first of which was delivered that year. Nine Beechcraft D17Ss were also delivered for air mail use, along with Grumman Widgeon seaplanes for use on the coast and in the Amazon region, where there were no runways but many rivers.

In the meantime, it was decided that it was necessary to create a unit to run the reception of the new combat planes and to train the crews. The *Agrupamento de Aviões de Adaptação* was thus created on 4 February 1942 at *Base Aérea de Fortaleza*, which was inaugurated on 21 May 1941 and where the *6 Regimento* was operating. The unit received 12 Curtiss P-36 Hawk fighters, two Douglas B-18 Bolo bombers, six B-25B Mitchells and six Curtiss P-40Es, with USAAF instructors. An idea by the Americans to send 20 A-20 Bostons from a batch built for the British was unsuccessful as the latter would not agree to give up the planes. The planes that were received were the first step towards modernization and, despite their main mission in the first months being training, together with the other FAB planes, they started maritime patrol missions.

Brazilian Air Force B-25B Mitchells.

A FAB AT-6G seen after the war.

A pilot in front of a FAB Curtiss P-40K.

To increase the presence of the force on the north-east coast, the *Base Aérea de Natal* was created in March 1942, forming, together with Recife, the *2º Zona Aérea*, under the command of Brigadier Eduardo Gomes, who tried to get as many planes as possible under his command, even using trainers like the Texans or liaison planes such as the D17Ss used by the *Correio Aéreo Nacional* of the FAB for patrol missions.

On 21 May, four days after the attack on the *Comandante Lyra*, the B-25B serialled 40-2245 (the recently received planes kept their US serials) took off from Fortaleza for a maritime patrol mission to search for the *Barbarigo*, commanded by 1st Lieutenant Henry Schwane of the USAAF, with Captains Affonso Celso Parreiras Horta and Oswaldo Pamplona Pinto as co-pilot and navigator respectively, 3rd Sergeant John Yates of the USAAF as bomber and 2nd Sergeant Morris Robinson of the USAAF the radio operator. After their patrol, they landed at Natal and continued the next day. On 22 May, the plane took off at 1215 and flew to Fernando de Noronha, passing over the island at 1330. At 1357 they saw the *Barbarigo* on the surface - it wasn't carrying any identification, so it was a hostile vessel. The B-25 was carrying 10 100lb general purpose bombs, with which it launched its attack from 300 metres. Two of the bombs fell close to the submarine and the others far off the stern. The submarine crew immediately opened fire on the B-25 with the gun on the bow, but failed to hit the plane. The *Barbarigo* increased its speed and started to turn, but remained on the surface, while the B-25 logged her position. As they saw the *Barbarigo* was not going down, they supposed she was damaged, so returned to base. The American forces there gave them two 320lb depth charges and they took off again at 1630, while another two B-25s did the same from Fortaleza, but it was impossible to find the submarine again. Despite not being successful, the Brazilian crews

A P-40 of the 2º Grupo Monoposto Monomotor at Recife in 1944.

The B-25B serialled 40-2309 received the Brazilian serial FAB 09 and here is seen at Natal in 1943, where the plane was used for operations against the German and Italian submarines. Archive Aparecido Camazano Alamino.

FAB personnel in front of the B-18 Bolo serialled 6300 and baptized Vira-Lata.

Focke Wulf *Weihe* of the Brazilian Air Force. An aircraft of this type was involved in an attack on an enemy U-Boat.

B-25B of the FAB.

The B-18 Bolo serialled FAB 7032 at Recife.

An A-28 Hudson at Campo dos Afonsos.

had started to have experience of war, and this day would become the Patrol Aviation Day, marking their baptism of fire.

Five days later, another encounter took place, involving the B-25 serialled 40-2263, which had taken off from Recife and flown over Fortaleza, commanded by Captain Parreiras Horta as pilot, with Lieutenant Cruz Whitington and 3rd Sergeants John Yates and Killan (whose first name remains unknown) - all of the USAAF - and Brazilian Sergeant Santiago. They attacked the Italian submarine *Capellini* 120 miles from Fortaleza, dropping one 320lb depth charge and three 500lb general purpose bombs at 0700, but they did not observed any result and the submarine submerged. Nevertheless, given the position of the vessel, in the afternoon the B-25 serialled 40-2255 was sent with Captain Pamplona Pinto, 1st Lieutenant Henry Schwane, 3rd Sergeant Bexgh (both of the USAAF) and Sergeant Venâncio. They found the submarine off Fortaleza and attacked her at 1630 with 500lb bombs, but again the airplane crew did not see any damage.

A Vultee Valiant. The FAB used this type to train new pilots during the war.

A P-40M in 1943.

Brazil at war

In June, the training of the crews on the new planes was considered finished and it was decided to deactivate the *Agrupamento de Aviões de Instrução*, sending one B-18 and five B-25s to the *Unidade Volante* (Flying Unit) of the *Base Aérea de Natal*. The P-40s went to the *Agrupamento de Aviões P-40* (P-40 Planes Group) at the same base of Fortaleza, until it was created the *Grupo Monoposto Monomotor* (GMM, Single Engine, Single Seat Group) on 11 November with the six P-40Es and nine P-40Ks recentrly received, together with three of the P-36As, while the other P-36s remained in Recife. The new planes were the first step in increasing the strength of fighter aviation, but they still lacked considerable power. At Recife, a group was kept with the three B-25Bs and the other B-18s, and in November they received the first two Lockheed A-28A Hudsons, with better capacity for antisubmarine warfare. They were from a batch originally built for the Royal Air Force, and were followed by another eight in December.

Meanwhile, after the incursions of the four Italian submarines and the attacks of the FAB, the German high command authorised their submarines on 4 July to attack any Brazilian ship they found, developing a plan to deploy 10 submarines, supported by the *U-460*, to attack ships all along the Brazilian coastline. In August, submarine *U-507* of Type IXC, under command of captain Harro Schacht, approached the Brazilian coast. It entered into action at 2012 on 15 August, sinking the *Baependi*, on which 270 people died, including a major part of the *7º Grupo de Artilharia de Dorso*, which was sailing to Recife. Only 36 people among the crew and passengers survived.

Two hours later, the *Araraquara* was sunk, causing 131 deaths among the 142 occupants, and at 0513 on 16 August the *U-507* sent the *Aníbal Benévolo* to the bottom of the sea, with only four survivors from 150 people aboard.

These attacks had a major impact on the Brazilians, with 550 people killed on three ships in just a matter of hours, but the most successful

The B-25B serialled FAB-10 (s/n 40-2310) of the Agrupamento de Aviões de Adaptação.

Vultee V-11 of the Brazilian Air Force. The type was used until 1949 but, since more modern types were received during the war, they were relegated to secondary missions.

raid by a German submarine on the Brazilian coast had not stopped yet. On the morning of 17 August, *U-507* sank the *Itagiba*, killing 36 people, followed that afternoon by the *Arará*, which was going to help the *Itagiba*, with the death of 20 of its 35 crew members. The German U-Boat ended the day with the destruction, using its gun, of the *Jacira* barge, which was abandoned by its crew. In total, 610 people were killed in less than three days, leading to the announcement, five days later, of a state of war with the Axis countries, which was made official on 31 August. The *U-507* was unsuccessfully attacked on 18 August by a Catalina of VP-83, which dropped depth charges, and on 20 August another attack was made on a submerged submarine by the same squadron, but again in vain.

Despite starting to have more advanced models, all FAB aircraft, even the oldest and those used for training, were used on patrol missions. The next contact with a submarine, probably the *U-507*, was made on 26 August by the Vultee V-11GB-2 serialled 122, commanded by 1st Lieutenant Alfredo Gonçalves Corrêa, with Applicant Manoel Poener Mazeron and Sergeant Carlos Zeil, when they found the vessel emerging onto the surface about 90km off the coast of Ararangua, near Canoas Air Base. The plane dropped three 250lb bombs while flying low, and shrapnel from the explosions damaged the engine cowling, so they had to return to the mainland without verifying the result of the attack, making an emergency landing at Osório. That was the only attack performed by these planes which, nevertheless,

A P-40E of the Grupo Monoposto Monomotor in 1943.

The B-18 serialled FAB 6300. The Bolos were among the first bombers received during the war.

A Liberator of VB-107, of the US Navy, over the South Atlantic.

The submarine *U-848* under attack by the PB4Y Liberator of VB197, serialled B-12, on 5 November 1943. The submarine was sunk with the loss of the entire crew.

The Martin PBM-3C Mariner, baptized Nickle Boat and serialled 74-P-5, was responsible for sinking both *U-128* and *U-513* off the Brazilian coast.

kept performing reconnaissance missions until more aircraft were received for this task during 1943. The *U-507*, after sinking a Swedish merchant ship, went across to the African coast, returning to Brazil some months later.

Among the planes inherited from the Army and Navy, the Fw-58 *Weihe* also performed reconnaissance, and the fleet was expanded by two transport versions received from the *Sindicato Cóndor* airline and the last batch of 10 built at the Galeão factory, delivered on 12 December 1942, making a total of 28 *Weihe*s for the FAB. For antisubmarine missions, the planes were modified with racks under the fuselage to carry 250lb depth charges and were equipped with a Browning 7.62mm machine gun on the nose and one on the dorsal position, replacing the original MG.15. However, despite flying many hours over the sea and spotting several submarines, they could not make any successful attacks.

Some patrol missions were also performed with the Vought V-65 Corsair, NA-44 and 72, among other models, armed with small bombs and machine guns.

More units

Meanwhile, in September 1942, convoys of merchantmen were organised, escorted by Navy ships and covered by FAB planes. With the arrival of eight extra Hudsons, on 27 December, the *Grupo de Aviões Bimotores* (GAB) was created at Recife, including the B-25s, A-28s and B-18s already there. On 5 November the *Base Aérea de*

US Navy Martin PBM-3 Mariners of VPB-211 flying over the statue of Christ the Redeemer in Rio de Janeiro.

A FAB Lockheed Hudson.

B-25Bs were intensively used on antisubmarine missions despite not being prepared for such a role.

Salvador was created, with a single NA-44, but by the beginning of 1943 seven A-28As were added; in January of that year another 16 examples arrived, followed by another one in March, while an extra one remained in the United States for use by the Brazilian officers who were receiving the planes in the USA, totalling 28 examples.

On 3 March 1943, another GAB was created at Natal, with three A-28As, together with the B-18 and the three B-25s already there. At that time, three A-28As were also sent to *Base Aérea de Fortaleza* and six remained at the *Unidade Volante do Galeão* in Rio de Janeiro. Three more were sent to Canoas and three others to Santa Cruz Air Base, created on 16 January 1943 from the basis of *Aeroporto Bartolomeu de Gusmão*, about 25km from Rio de Janeiro. That airport was used by the *Graf Zeppelin* and *Hindenburg* on their flights to Brazil and had a huge hangar for them, which was transferred to the FAB.

The transition to the Hudson was easy for the pilots, because the air force already had 10 Lodestars for transport, which were very similar.

US forces

The operations of VP-83 continued for the rest of the year at a very high level. On 3 November, the Catalina serialled P-10, commanded by Lieutenant George Waugh, detected a submarine that was probably the Italian *Da Vinci*. Waugh dropped four depth charges and the gunners fired at the submarine, but it submerged and escaped. On 13 December, another attack took place against *U-126*, but the Catalina of Lieutenant Gerard Bradford missed with two Mk-17 and two Mk-29 depth charges. On the next day, the plane commanded by Lieutenant W.L. Wall attacked *U-174* and damaged the vessel with depth charges, but the Germans escaped. Four hours later, another plane, commanded by Lieutenant Commander Bertram Prueher, attacked *U-161* with depth charges, causing heavy damage to the submarine. On the following morning, the Catalina P-9 of Lieutenant Frederick Andretta dropped a Mk-17 depth charge when the *U-161* was diving, but she escaped again.

On 17 December, the plane of Lieutenant Bradford found *U-176*, but the submarine dived before an attack could be made. However, the Catalina stayed in the area and half an hour later the submarine emerged, so they pressed the attack with three depth charges, causing heavy damage.

1943, growing in combat

By the beginning of the year, the organization of the FAB was as follows:

1º Regimento:

Campo dos Afonsos: Aviation School, with 50 Vultee BT-15s, 40 Fairchild PT-19s, 10 Beech C-18Ss, the remaining Fw-44Js, Stearmans and Muniz M-9s and some other models.

Base Aérea do Galeão: nine Fw-58 *Weihe*, one Vought V-65B Corsair, three NA-72s, four Grumman Widgeons, 11 NA-46s and five A-28 Hudsons. During the year, the Unidade Volante

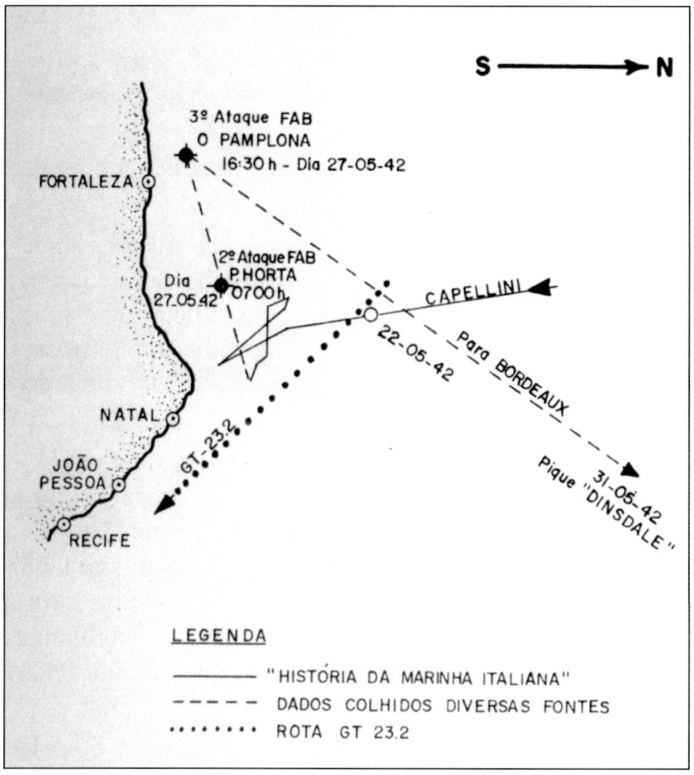

Route of the submarine *Capellini* off Brazil.

The crew of the B-25B which made the first attack against a submarine. From left to right: Captain Affonso Parreiras Horta, USAAF First Lieutenant Henry Schwane and Captain Oswaldo Pamplona Pinto.

do Galeão received the first three PBY-5 Catalinas and seven A-28 Hudsons.

Base Aérea de Santa Cruz: 20 Vultee V-11s, eight V-65B Corsairs and three A-28 Hudsons.

2º Corpo de Base Aérea:

Base Aérea de São Paulo: six Vultee V-65s.

Base Aérea de Santos: four Fw-58 *Weihe*, received in November 1942.

3º Regimento:

Base Aérea de Canoas: six Vultee V-65s, three Vultee V-11s, four NA-72s and one Fw-58 *Weihe*. In January 1943, they also received three Lockheed A-28 Hudsons, which served with that unit until December 1944.

4º Corpo de Base Aérea:

Base Aérea de Belo Horizonte: No air units of any importance.

5º Regimento:

Base Aérea de Curitiba: six Vultee V-65s, eight Boeing 256s and two Fw-58 *Weihe*.

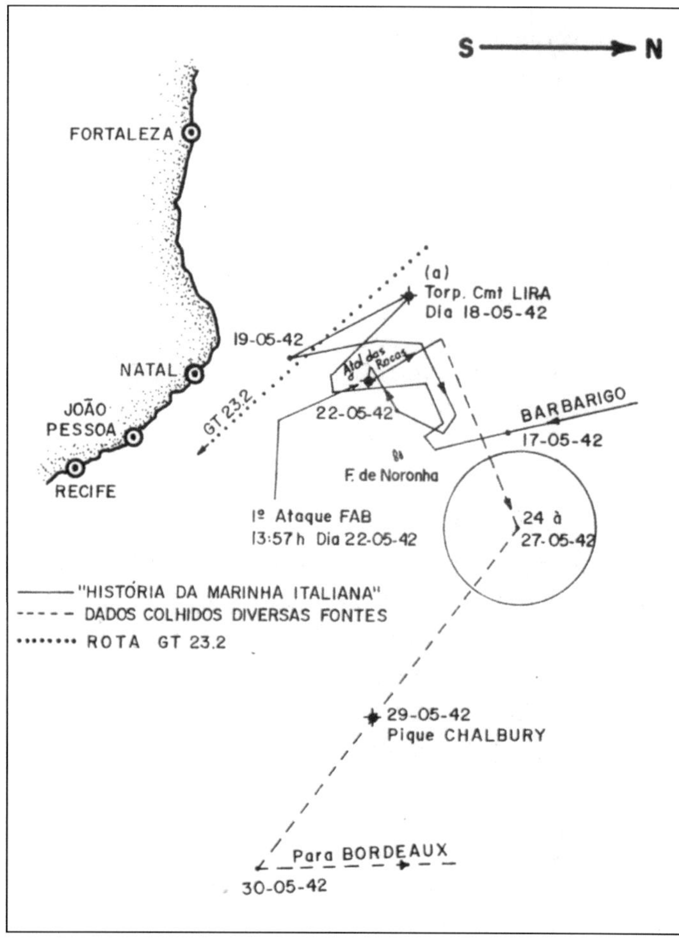

Route of the submarine *Barbarigo* off Brazil.

6º Corpo de Base Aérea:

Base Aérea de Fortaleza: Grupo Bimotor, with three A-28A Hudsons and three AT-6B Texans.

Base Aérea de Recife: Grupo de Aviões Bimotores, with six B-25B Mitchells, two B-18 Bolos and four AT-6B Texans.

7º Corpo de Base Aérea:

Base Aérea de Belém: four Grumman Widgeons, and during the year they received three PBY-5 Catalinas.

8º Corpo de Base Aérea:

Base Aérea de Campo Grande: No air units of any importance.

Base Aérea de Natal:

Grupo de Aviões Bimotores, with one B-18 Bolo, three B-25Bs, three A-28As and three AT-6B Texans.Grupo Monoposto Monomotor, with three P-36 Hawks and 15 P-40Ks.

14º Corpo de Base Aérea:

Base Aérea de Florianópolis: one PBY-5 Catalina received during 1943, two *Weihe* received in November 1942 and two Widgeons arrived in December 1942.

Base Aérea de Salvador: started the year with three NA-44s, and later received seven A-28 Hudsons.

Brazilian operations against submarines

The growth in intensity of anti-submarine operations in the North Atlantic, and the greater support given to the Allies by Latin American nations, led to an increase in the presence of submarines in the South Atlantic.

In May 1943, the submarines *U-128* and *U-154* approached the Brazilian coast, and on the 27th *U-154* launched its first attack against convoy BT-14 near Cabo São Roque, after being supplied by *U-515*. Meanwhile, *U-182*, *U-195* and *U-197* approached Ascension Island,

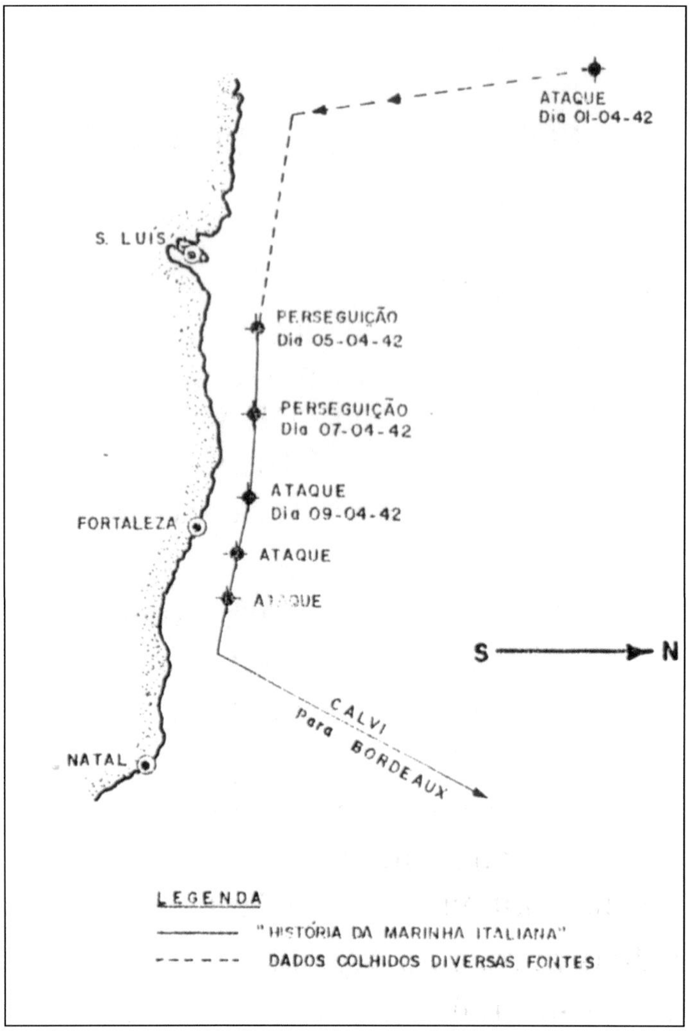

Route of the submarine *Calvi* near Brazil.

One of the FAB B-25Bs.

Curtiss P-40Ns of the FAB in flight.

followed by *U-180*, *U-513* and *U-199*.

To combat these submarines, patrol missions were intensified during the year and the Brazilian Air Force started to receive the first seven Consolidated PBY-5 Catalinas, three of them destined for Galeão, three for Belém and one for Florianópolis, serialled PA-01 to PA-06 and P-4. The crews of those planes, like those of the Hudsons, regularly trained with the submarines of the *Marinha Brasileira*.

The first action involving the German submarines in 1943 was the sinking of the *Brasilóide* on 18 February by the *U-518*, four days after the U-Boat was unsuccessfully attacked by the B-25 serialled 45 of *Grupo de Aviões Bimotores* at Recife. On the following day, the NA-44 serialled 07 of *Base Aérea de Salvador* attacked a target they could not identify; the pilot, Major Aquino, thought it was a submarine, but the bombs missed their target.

On 2 March, the Italian submarine *Barbarigo* sank the *Affonso Penna*, killing 94 people. This was followed by an attack carried out by 1st Lieutenant Franqueira's NA-44 serialled 08, also from *Base Aérea de Salvador*, which was protecting a convoy near Canavieiras on 22 March. The pilot, after flying for 10-15 minutes, saw a merchant ship on the horizon at 0745 and went to identify it. As he arrived, he saw a trail 2-3km behind the ship, quickly idenfying the periscope of a submarine. He immediately attacked it, dropping general purpose bombs which fell near the periscope. The submarine dived and it was not possible to identify if it was damaged. After orbiting the area for a while, the NA-44 returned to base, while two A-28 Hudsons were sent to hunt for the submarine but could not find it.

The next plane that made an attack on a submarine also departed from Salvador. The A-28 Hudson serialled 75, under the command of 1st Lieutenant Ivo Gastaldoni, took off at 0940 on 5 April to protect convoy BT-19 that was sailing to Trinidad. As the plane was approaching the convoy, at 1050, crew member Sergeant Angelo informed the pilot that he could see something suspect below the right wing. The pilot tilted the plane and, from a height of 2,500ft, identified the trail left by the mast of a periscope, so he immediately began an attack. Because of their height, the pilot could not put the plane in a good position for the first bomb run, for which he dived, but they could clearly see the submarine, which was sailing 20km behind the convoy with a heading of 080°. The pilot turned and started a second attack, from an angle of 45° over the submarine, and at 100ft dropped four depth charges. According to Lieutenant Gastaldoni:

> The impact was seen a short distance from the periscope, which was still visible, and the foam provoked by the explosion surrounded the whole submarine. The vessel kept sailing at the same depth, making a steep turn to the left and leaving an oil trail for about a minute. After that it came almost to the surface and immediately disappeared. Then we saw three life vests and a red life raft on the surface, plus a piece of yellow wood, like a skull, and more oil poured to the surface. I flew over the place for an hour, then moved away 30km to identify a merchant ship coming from the south, and when I returned I found only the piece of wood, a big oil stain of 100 by 300 metres and another one, less accentuated, of 300 by 300 metres. Finally, I landed at the base at 1415 after a flight of four hours and 35 minutes.

Two P-40Ks of the Grupo Monoposto Monomotor of Natal in 1943.

A P-40 of the Agrupamento de Aviões P-40 in 1943.

A P-40K of the Grupo Monoposto Monomotor at Natal in 1943.

Unfortunately, it was not possible to confirm the submarine that had been attacked nor the result of the attack, but it seems the vessel was sunk. Some days after the attack, several mutilated bodies were found on the coast. Shortly after that date, the submarines *U-519*, *U-553* and *U-337* were contacted for the last time, and were later declared lost.

On 8 May, one of the B-18 Bolos, serialled 6300 and based at Recife, took off to protect the tanker *Motocarline*, which had been unsuccessfully attacked with torpedoes on the previous day. The plane was manned by Lieutenant Zamir de Barros Pinto, Aspirant Geraldo Labarthe Lebre and Sergeants Castro and Jayme. According to the report of Lieutenant Barros Pinto, they took off at 0825:

Line up of Fw-58 *Weihe* planes.

A P-40E of the Grupo Monoposto Monomotor.

A *Weihe* of the Brazilian Navy in flight before 1941.

To the south-east of Recife, 40km from the coast, a convoy of four ships was seen at 0840. At 0908, a US destroyer was seen sailing near the city of Cabo. The *Motocarline* was located 80km from Maceió, with a course of 190º. At 1100, the destroyer was 300km from the tanker with a heading of 180º. At 1155 the protection of the tanker was finished, when it was near the mouth of the river located to the north of San Miguel de Campos, 90km from the coast. Then we received the order to fly for 30 minutes over a position 95km from Ponta de Pedras, we headed at 65º and at 1210 saw a submarine sailing on the surface at high spead, with a heading of 240º. Before the plane reached the vertical over the submarine, she dived, showing the periscope for a while. Two depth charges and a training bomb were dropped, falling to the front of the foam left by the submarine, and from the water appeared a big oil stain. The B-18 kept flying over the place for one hour and the continued to the *Motocarline*. By then, the destroyer was sailing 200km to the north of the tanker. We returned to the place of the attack and at 1400 we saw a Catalina overflying that position, and at 1430 we started the return to Maceió for refuelling, landing at 1530.

The B-18 took off again at 1650 and returned to the same base at 1755. The submarine was the *U-154*, which, despite being damaged, survived, but could not sink the *Motocarline*, which they were hunting.

On 25 June, a Fw-58 *Weihe* performed the only attack made by this bomber model against a submarine, when the plane commanded by Lieutenant Georg Bungner, with Petty Officer Raul, took off from Galeão Air Base on a patrol mission to the area around Vitória. About 30 miles from the coast of Cabo Frío, the petty officer informed the pilot he could see a strange vessel, so they descended and identified it as a submarine. The submarine immediately changed heading and started an emergency dive. The *Weihe* was carrying a 300lb depth charge, which was activated to be dropped, but when they arrived over the location they only saw the foam left by the submarine. The charge was dropped and its explosion was verified, but no damage to the submarine was seen and the plane returned to base. The submarine attacked was the *U-513*, which was operating near Rio de Janeiro and at that time was on surface together with the *U-199*, which wasn't seen by the *Weihe*.

Five days later, a curious situation happened with another *Weihe*. The same pilot, together with trainee Karl Heinz Eberius, both of German origin, was flying near Caraguatatuba, near the entrance to São Sebastião harbour channel, over two isolated merchant vessels, which were not part of any convoy, when the smaller one of them was torpedoed. The other ship, showing a US flag, opened fire with its stern gun on the place from where the torpedo had come. The *Weihe* made some overflights but saw nothing. The submarine was again the *U-513*. Because of the German origin of both crew members, some people of the FAB suspected them and their statement that they did not see the submarine, but the force never doubted their report.

Submarines sunk by the US Navy

Depsite the FAB being re-equipped at a good pace, it still lacked enough capacity to patrol the huge coastline of Brazil, so during 1942 and 1943 the United States started to deploy units to several air

Vultee V-11s over Rio de Janeiro.

bases, as part of Task Force 44. In December 1942, a VP-74 and VP-94 Squadron arrived at Natal, the first belonging to Patrol Wing 11, which was equipped with Martin PBM-3 Mariners and supported by the tender USS *Humboldt*.

Their first encounter with the enemy was on 6 January 1943, when a plane commanded by Ensign Herbert Boyce saw the trail of a submarine under the surface and then the submarine itself, dropping four depth charges but being unable to confirm any damage to the vessel. In the following month, they received a PBM-3C to increase their capabilities, and on 24 February they had another encounter, when the plane commanded by Ensign W.O. Barnard found a submarine at periscope depth attacking a merchant vessel. When the Mariner was on the bomb run, the submarine emerged and opened fire on it, and although the plane pressed its attack it could not confirm the result, as the crew lost sight of the submarine after that.

On 16 January, another unit joined the effort, with the arrival at Natal of VP-94, of Patrol Wing 11, led by Lieutenant Commander. H.R. Swanson.

1943 was the most active year for antisubmarine warfare, including in the South Atlantic. Besides the Brazilian forces, which were re-equipping little by little, US forces performed constant patrol missions from bases on the Brazilian coast, with more modern material and greater experience, leading to an increase in success. This was reflected on 6 January 1943, when *U-164* was sunk near Pernambuco with four Mk-23 depth charges launched from the Catalina serialled P-2, commanded by Lieutenant William Ford, of VP-83 Squadron. According to Ford's report on the mission:

Line up of FAB P-40s at Canoas Air Base, near Porto Alegre, in 1945.

P-40M of the 2º Grupo de Caça at Natal in 1944.

We were flying at 5,600ft when Billy Goodell, who made two visual contacts previously, reported he had seen something in the middle of the sea. As soon as I saw the submarine I turned 90 degrees to port and put the propeller and throttle back. There was a small cloud between the submarine and the plane. The indicated speed was 184 knots with a descent rate of 2,000ft per minute. When we were at about three to four miles from the target, I pulled to full power and started to approach the submarine, who apparently hadn't see us, with an angle of about 60 degrees.

The submarine maintained course and the Catalina approached at about 36ft until the co-pilot dropped the depth charges, the submarine being raised out of the water by the explosion and breaking into two pieces. Only two men survived.

The other submarine that was worrying Allied forces in Brazil was the *U-507*, and great efforts were made to find it. Meanwhile, on 12 January, the Catalina serialled 10 with Lieutenant Ludwig was sent from Natal to Belém to protect a convoy. Less than two hours after take-off, they found three life rafts from a sunk merchant ship, and through the Aldis signal lamp they were informed the survivors had food and water. After confirming their position and informing Natal about them, the Catalina resumed its trip to Belém. On the next day, they were informed that a submarine was following the convoy and took off in the morning to protect the ships. According to Ludwig:

Before take-off, all of us, including the co-pilot, Lieutenant Mearl Taylor, the navigator, Ensign Harry Holt, the radio operators and two lateral gunners, whose names were Merrick and Thurston, revised our plan. We would not use the intervalometer when we dropped the depth charges, as there were some cases when they stayed on the pylons. We would fly at about 6,000ft, using the cover

Two P-40Ms of Base Aérea de Salvador in 1943.

of the clouds to hide us as much as possible. If we performed an attack I would drop two charges using the button to do it manually, to drop the two outer ones, one on each side. Mearl, on the co-pilot seat, would drop the other on the right and Harry, standing between us, the last one. If we were lucky they would fall at intervals of one to two seconds.

Gerhofer [one of the mechanics] would inform the base sending a clear message that we were attacking. The two gunners on the sides would operate the .50 machine guns and fire after receiving the order, from me or Mearl. We would not use the .30 machine gun in the nose. We would fly to a place 50 miles ahead of the course of the convoy and then go on a straight line to where it was. This way we would be seeing the sea with the sun on our back and with more chance to have the surprise on our side.

After taking off after sunset, when they were arpproaching Natal they found the *U-507*. Ludwig continued:

Nobody said anything when, on our route, we passed her to my side. Whatever it was, luck or lack of sleep in the last few days, or still being clouds between us and the sea, the truth is that I didn't see her. Shortly after, Mearl stretched from where he was seated and said: 'Does that thing there look like a patrol vessel?' I looked once and immediately answered: 'That's a submarine!'

Then everything happened at once. The throttle was reduced, the nose dived, the alarm called action stations, and the depth charges were prepared. Harry Holt came to the front and accommodated himself between Mearl and me. Shortly after we were diving at more than 200 knots. We were approaching the submarine from the front and, until then, there was no signal they had seen us. Time seemed to stand still, but in a few seconds, were were flying at 1,200ft over the sea. The submarine had seen us and was trying to dive. We reduced the dive, but the nose was still pointing downwards. The throttle was pulled to maintain our speed. Mearl was ready to activate the release system of the right side; Harry was on the left. I had my hand on the mechanism to drop the charges. We were almost there and now the submarine only had the turret over the surface. We were 100ft over the water and gliding. I pushed the button to drop the charges, looking to a point exactly in front of the turret. Mearl and Harry then dropped their weapons at the exact moment.

Fortunately, the four charges fell, because at that point we were flying at only 25ft over the sea's surface and the loss of about 1,000 kilos helped the plane to recover some altitude and level out. In a very short time we were turning to the left and climbing. I looked back, and what a vision! It looked like the Niagara Falls upside down: a tremendous wall of water erupted on the sea, in a single four column. While we circled over the area we dropped some smoke markers, but we didn't see anything from the submarine

A P-40K of 2º Grupo Monoposto Monomotor of Recife, still with USAAF serial, in 1943.

besides the foam left by the depth charges. Harry Holt went to the radio room, calculated our position and informed the base about the attack. I asked over the intercom: 'Does anyone see the convoy?' I think it was the second mechanic of the plane, Aviation Mechanic W. Dickinson, who answered: 'We passed over it about five minutes ago, before starting the attack.'

I gave the command to Meark to head in the direction of the convoy and then to the lateral bubble windows, asking the gunners: 'Did you see the depth charges hitting the target?'

'Yes.'

'Did any of them jump after the initial impact on the water?'

'No.'

'They seemed to hit the submarine?'

'Right in front of the turret.'

'What do you think about the attack?'

'We thought we were going to crash against the submarine.'

'Good, very close, but keep your eyes on the smoke the whole time as we will return and inform the convoy.'

The cruiser USS *Omaha* went to the scene of the attack but found no trace of the submarine. Despite it originally being thought that the vessel was only damaged, it was later discovered that *U-507* was completely destroyed in the action.

In March 1943, the US Navy created Fleet Air Wing 16 (FAW-16) from the three units based at Natal, as part of the Fourth Fleet, as the forces in the South Atlantic were now called. The wing was under the command of Captain Rossmore D. Lyon and, despite initially having its headquarters in Norfolk, Virginia, in April they were moved to Natal and in July to Recife. The squadrons under their command were VP-83 and VP-94 with PBY-5A Catalinas, and VP-74 with Mariners.

In the meantime, in March, three Mariners of VP-74 started to operate from Aratu Base, in Salvador, and were joined by the others, apart from one, in April.

On 15 April, a PBY-5A Catalina of VP-83, piloted by Ensign T.E. Robertson, while searching for blockade-runners travelling from Japan to Germany, spotted the Italian submarine *Archimede* while they were returning from their mission. Navigator Ensign Eugene Morrison was going to the nose of the plane when Seaman 2nd Class Earl J. Kloss saw the submarine and Morrison identified it, informing Robertson. As they had flown over the submarine, they started a turn to the left and immediately the guns on the submarine opened fire. The pilot attempted to bomb the submarine, trying to force the gunners to seek cover, but the *Archimede* started diving. Robertson then dived from 7,300ft with 60 degrees of inclination and reached 245 knots. When the submarine disappeared, as the Catalina was at 2,000ft, the pilot dropped the four charges. Immediately after, the submarine surfaced and started turning to starboard for about 20 minutes and moving very slowly. The guns on the submarine opened fire on the Catalina again, and Robertson informed four other patrol planes that were in

The sole surviving *Weihe* in the world at the Museu Aeroespacial of Campo dos Afonsos.

A *Weihe* while in service with the FAB. The airplanes received US-built machine guns for their defensive armament.

the area of the Italians' presence.

The Catalina piloted by Lieutenant G. Bradford, Jr. arrived an hour later and dropped another four charges from a height of 50ft, hitting the ship in the middle, making four further passes and strafing the vessel, which was still firing its guns at the aircraft. The *Archimede* sank a few minutes later, but 20 crewmen escaped into the sea. The Catalinas dropped three life rafts to them, but only one was rescued on 27 May, with just a sole survivor, Giuseppe Lococo.

To increase the capacity of FAW-16, VB-127 Squadron, equipped with Lockheed PV-1 Venturas, arrived at Natal on 10 May, followed a few days later by VB-129, also with Venturas. VP-83 returned to Norfolk with five planes on the day VB-127 arrived, delivering their other three Catalinas to VP-94, which remained with 12 planes. This squadron converted to the PB4Y-1 Liberator, receiving 15 aircraft, and changed its name to VB-107, returning to Brazil in July.

On 14 May, a Catalina of VP-94 found *U-128* close to convoy BT-13, being the first contact of that squadron with an enemy vessel, but the submarine submerged before the Catalina could perform the attack. Two days later, a Marine P-2 of VP-74 took off at 1120, with Lieutenant Gibbs in command, to patrol an area to the north-east of their base at Aratu, Salvador. At 1351 they reported spotting an object on the sea's surface about 15 miles away, and shortly after identified it as a submarine. Gibbs manoeuvred to put his plane behind some clouds and headed for the submarine. When they were close to it, the submarine dived, but when they arrived over where it had submerged they dropped six Mk-44 depth charges, without damaging the submarine.

The submarine tried to chase convoy BT-13 during the night, without success, despite only being about 12 miles from it. The presence of the Mariners flying over the convoy forced the submarine to remain at a distance. On 17 May, the Mariners kept patrolling the

Liberator 107-B-4, baptized Macahyba Maiden, one of the planes that sank *U-848*.

One of the FAB NA-46s used for training before the arrival of the Texans.

The Mariner 74-P-5 attacking *U-128*. The depth charges can be seen falling below the plane.

area until Mariner 74-P-6, piloted by Lieutenant Davis, saw the trail of a submarine on the surface, about 18 miles away. At the same time, Mariner 74-P-5, piloted by Lieutenant Harold Carey, detected the submarine with its radar at a distance of 28 miles. Carey stated in his report of the mission:

> Using the binoculars I could see a submarine on the surface and ordered an attack. Ensign Smolsnik, who was the usual pilot of 74-P-5, was in the pilot seat, so I prepared the bombs. Immediately after the beginning of the bomb run the submarine started to dive. Then we noted that the 74-P-6, of VP-74, was entering to attack to our front, at about two miles.

The crew of *U-128* saw the planes approaching and started to dive, but a mechanical failure delayed the manoeuvre and it only went down when 74-P-6 was on its bomb run. Davis stated:

> The submarine, sailing at about 15 knots, started to dive when our plane was less than two miles away and disappeared when we were three-quarters of a mile from it. Crossing her path at an angle of 50° and about 50-70 metres ahead of where the swirl formed on the water, we dropped the Mk-44 depth charges at an altitude of 50ft, as in the manual.

The pilot started to climb and turn to watch the result of the attack, and kept flying over the area. The submarine was seriously damaged by the depth charges and could not escape. Davis continued:

> In the middle of the second circle over the area of the attack, the tail gunner informed through the intercom that the submarine was returning to the surface to starboard. It was on a reciprocal heading and its course apparently turned hard to the right. She was about a quarter of a mile from where we attacked. We went to a position from where we could start a bomb run to attack with our machine guns, but we saw the PBM number 5 entering to attack and we turned to free the area. We went to fly in parallel and photographed their attack. Immediately we turned left and we followed them, on what was the first of a series of attacks by the two planes.

The crew of *U-128* was caught by surprise by the second Mariner and their commander decided to head towards the Brazilian coast, as he realised there was no escape for them.

Mariner 74-P-5 made its attack at just 100ft and on a heading of 45° from that of the submarine, and Carey released the depth charges while Smolsnik flew the plane, seriously damaging the submarine. The Mariners performed several passes strafing the submarine, which attempted to dive about four times, but only once managed to do so, leaving part of the turret still above the surface. After the fifth strafing attack, the crew of 74-P-5 saw an explosion on the submarine, which

The *U-604* under attack by the Ventura of Lieutenant Commander Thomas Davies on 30 July 1943.

The Lockheed PV-1 Ventura 129-B-3 of VB-129.

was probably the ammunition of the guns exploding. The strafing passes continued, impeding any chance of defence by the submarine. With other planes and ships approaching, at 0952 the submarine stopped, the crew attempting to inform the planes they were surrendering and starting to abandon ship. At 1101, 74-P-6 dropped a life raft to about 10 men who were in the water behind the submarine. Shortly after, the destroyers USS *Moffett* and USS *Jouett* appeared and fired their guns on the damaged submarine, hitting it four times before it sunk. The USS *Moffett* recovered 51 survivors from the 54-strong crew, but four were seriously wounded and died on the destroyer.

When the presence of a submarine (the *U-513*) was detected near Rio de Janeiro on 21 July, four Catalinas of VP-94 were deployed to Santos Dumont airport in that city, supported by the tender USS *Barnegat*. Also at that time, VB-127 Squadron was deployed to Fortaleza to patrol the northern coast of Brazil. With the arrival of VB-107, there were now five US Navy squadrons in Brazil: VP-74 was at Aratu, with some Mariners deployed in Rio de Janeiro; VB-94 at Natal, with planes deployed to Belém; VB-107 at Natal; VB-127 at Fortaleza; and VB-129 at Recife, although later transferred to Ipitanga Base in Salvador.

July was very active for the German submarines along the Brazilian coast, but was also the most successful month for the Americans, starting with the sinking of the *U-590* on the 9th by a Catalina of VP-94, near the mouth of the Amazon River. The action started when several submarines were detected following convoys BT-18 and TJ-1. The first convoy was being protected by five Catalinas from Belém, and at 1235 the plane piloted by Lieutenant Frank F. Hare, who was searching the area around convoy TJ-1, saw *U-590* sailing on the surface. Hare started his attack, but when they were about a mile off the submarine, a bullet hit the cockpit and killed Hare and wounded the radio operator. The co-pilot, Lieutenant Phelps, assumed command and continued the attack, dropping two depth charges, but the submarine was not damaged. After flying over the area for half an hour, they left the submarine, which was still on the surface. When they left, another Catalina and a Liberator of VB-107 arrived in the area, but they could not find the submarine. The planes kept patrolling the area, and at 1424 the Catalina piloted by Lieutenant Stanley Auslander found the vessel emerging near Maracá Island, Amapá. The Catalina was at about 3,700ft in cloud cover when a gunner saw the submarine and Auslander dived and turned. As the Catalina approached, the submarine was on the surface. The plane prepared to attack, and when they were at just 150ft the co-pilot dropped the depth charges over the submarine and then made a turn to the left. The submarine disappeared after the explosions, all that remained being some debris and two men in the ocean. Despite catching two of the life vests dropped by the Catalina, they were never recovered.

This sinking was followed on the 19th by that of *U-513* near São Francisco do Sul by a Mariner of VP-74. The submarine was found

The Hudson serialled 41-47172 was donated to the FAB by the Fraternidade do Fole of Brazil.

View of the *U-199* from the US Navy Mariner which performed the first strike.

near Florianópolis, to the south of Brazil, when a radio transmission from her was detected. The Mariner 74-P-5, piloted by Lieutenant Roy Whitcomb, took off from Florianópolis, where it was supported by the USS *Barnegat*, and after a while detected the submarine on its radar. The submarine also spotted the Mariner when it was very close, and its gunners opened fire on the plane, but the 20mm gun soon jammed. The Mariner dropped four depth charges from 50ft, three of them causing severe damage to the submarine's hull and throwing the men in the turret and manning the guns into the water. Immediately after, the submarine sunk from the bow; the Mariner dropped two life rafts and some life vests for the survivors, seven of whom were recovered by the USS *Barnegat* that night.

On that same day, *U-662* was found by a USAAF B-18 Bolo while following convoy TF-2 near Cayenne, but the attack by the plane was unsuccessful. The submarine was attacked again, near Surinam, by a USAAF B-24 Liberator and on 20 July was found by a Catalina of VP-94 commanded by Lieutenant Auslander, who had departed Macapá at 1030. At 1341, one of the gunners found a vessel sailing five miles away to their left, and once Auslander realised it was a submarine he started to dive from 4,000ft and turned towards her. The Catalina started its bomb run despite heavy fire from *U-662* and, while the side gunners strafed the vessel, the co-pilot dropped the depth charges from 100ft, but missed the target by around 10 metres. Auslander informed the escort of the convoy and remained flying 5,000ft over the submarine, waiting for the ships. While a destroyer was approaching, at 1445 the submarine dived and escaped.

At 0230 on 21 July, the Catalina P-4 took off from Belém to relieve the P-7 in the protection of convoy TJ-2 and arrived on station three hours later. At 0602, they saw *U-662* near the mouth of the Amazon River about three miles from them. The Catalina was flying at 1,200ft and 95 knots when the pilot, Lieutenant Roland, prepared for attack and headed towards the submarine. The ship opened fire, but the 20mm guns jammed, despite the guns managing to hit the Catalina several times. At 75ft, the plane dropped the depth charges, but one remained, while the side gunners fired on the turret. Two of the charges exploded beneath the submarine and caused heavy damage inside. The submarine sank immediately, but five men survived on rafts launched by the Catalina, being rescued by USS *Siren* 16 days later, one of them dying on the rescue ship.

One day later, a Liberator piloted by Lieutenant Commander Turner, of VB-107, was performing a training flight when, at 2125, it found *U-598*, which had just arrived in the area from Germany. Turner dropped six depth charges over the vessel shortly after the submarine submerged. He informed his base and kept patrolling the area, while the Liberator serialled 107-B-8, commanded by Lieutenant John Burton, was approaching, and at 2252 dropped the remaining two depth charges, but caused no damage. The 107-B-8 arrived shortly after, followed by the 107-B-5, and circled over the submarine and tried to keep it under the surface until they ran out of oxygen and were forced to return to the surface during the daytime. The planes were relieved after midnight by the 107-B-12 of Lieutenant Baldwin, and at 0635 the plane saw the submarine emerging again six miles from them. The Liberator performed an attack with depth charges, causing some damage to the vessel, especially to the engines, which stopped working. Two other Liberators - the 107-B-6 with Lieutenant Waugh and 107-B-8 with Lieutenant Ford - were performing training flights at that moment, as the crews had recently arrived from Norfolk, and went to the place of the attack. The submarine commander realised that, without the engines, there was no escape, so dropped two life rafts and ordered his men to abandon the ship before the second attack came. While they were boarding the rafts, the plane of Waugh attacked, but flew so low that the explosions of the depth charges hit the plane, which crashed into the sea and disintegrated. The plane of Ford attacked in a dive and passed through the water columns raised by the former attack, dropped their depth charges and hit the submarine, which sank immediately. One of the rafts was sucked down by the sinking vessel and some of the survivors who were in the water caught two rafts that had emerged from the destroyed Liberator and inflated automatically, but one of the rafts was lost without trace. In the end, only two crew members of *U-598* were rescued by a US destroyer.

Further action took place on 30 July. First, a Ventura of VB-129, commanded by Lieutenant Commander Thomas Davies, found the submarine *U-604* and went to attack her, diving and reaching 265 knots. *U-604* opened fire with its guns and the Ventura did the same with the forward machine guns. As they flew just ahead of the turret, they dropped four Mk-74 depth charges from 50ft. Despite the charges not causing much initial damage, when the submarine started an emergency dive, one of the bombs, which had probably stuck somewhere on the submarine, exploded near the stern. *U-604* dived, but shortly after returned to the surface, the Ventura strafing the turret while it was partially under water. The submarine dived and turned, appearing later and sailing back with the stern above the surface, and then dived again, disappearing. The Ventura crew, convinced they had sunk the submarine, returned to base. In fact, the submarine was very seriously damaged and, unable to return to France, received orders to meet *U-591* to transfer the crew and then sink the vessel.

Also on 30 July, a Ventura of VB-127, commanded by Lieutenant Walter Young, who was protecting convoy TJ-2, saw on the radar the submarine *U-591* near Recife. The plane was at 4,000ft, and they approached until they saw the vessel 12 miles away. At 1228, the Ventura dived and attacked the surprised submarine, dropping six

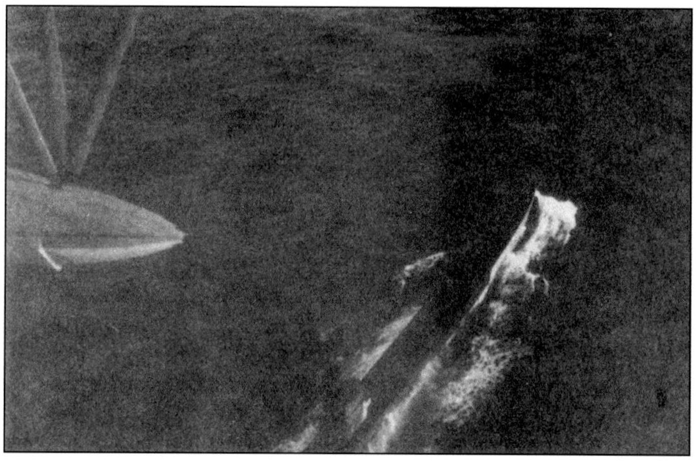

The US Navy Mariner flying over *U-199* during the attack.

The PBY-5, baptized Arará, which sank *U-199*.

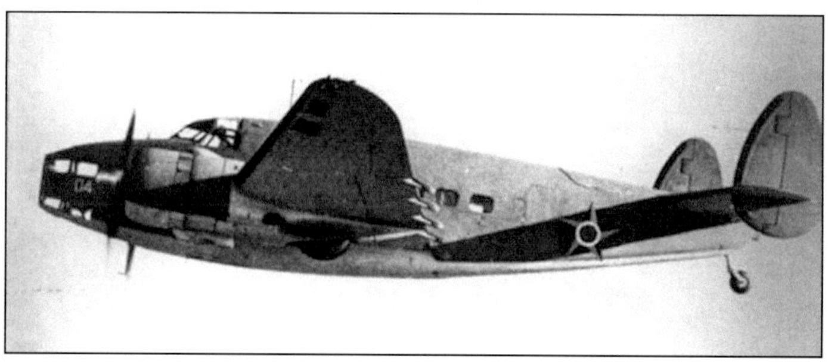

The Hudson serialled FAB-04 in flight.

Mk-44 depth charges from 50ft and at a speed of 260 knots. One of the charges made a hole in the hull, while another destroyed the turret. The ship lost its electrical power and the commander realised it was doomed, so he gave the order to abandon ship. The survivors caught a raft launched by the Ventura, and 28 of them, from a crew of 49, were later rescued by the destroyer USS *Saucy*.

A US Navy PBM-3 Mariner together with the tender USS *Rockaway* off the Brazilian coast.

As *U-591* was sunk, the rendezvous of *U-604* was then planned with *U-185*. While the two submarines were communicating, on 3 August, their position was located by the Allies, who detected the communications, and planes were sent out on patrol. A Liberator of VB-107 piloted by Lieutenant Commander Prueher, the squadron commander, found the submarine and attacked with Mk-47 depth charges where it had dived. Despite an oil stain being seen, she was not damaged in this attack. When night fell, the submarine emerged, but started to receive fire from USS *Moffett*'s guns, so the submarine dived again and had to avoid depth charges launched by the destroyer. The Liberator returned to Recife for fuel and depth charges, and took off again at 1735, finding *U-185* with the radar. Despite the dark, they saw the submarine tracers firing on the plane and attacked the vessel with machine guns and four depth charges. The Liberator then attacked again, dropping the remaining two depth charges from 175ft but missing the target. They returned to base having received 23 hits from the guns of the submarine, which escaped undamaged, but with an injured crew member.

The rendezvous would now also include *U-172* and was planned for 8 August, but intense air activity forced a delay until the 11th, when *U-185* and *U-604* located each other and were later joined by *U-172*. In the meantime, Lieutenant Commander Prueher took off and appeared over the submarines shortly after the arrival of *U-172*, dropping depth charges on the damaged *U-604*, but causing no damage. Prueher's machine guns wounded several of the crew of *U-172* and hit the guns, leaving the submarine undefended, so her commander decided to dive. *U-185* started to protect the *U-604* and fired upon the Liberator, which dived from 1,200ft for another attack but crashed into the sea, killing its entire crew.

After transferring the crew to *U-185*, *U-604* was sunk. Fourteen crew members had died during the actions, with 31 survivors.

5

THE SINKING OF SUBMARINE *U-199*

By mid 1943 the activity of German submarines off the Brazilian coast had grown considerably, because it had become more difficult to attack convoys in the North Atlantic due to the greater presence of Allied forces, which now also had tools such as radars on board their planes and acoustic torpedoes, etc. The German submarines that went to operate to Brazil were divided into areas: *U-510*, *U-466*, *U-590*, *U-662* and *U-653* were near the mouth of the Amazon River and in the Caribbean; *U-604*, *U-598*, *U-591* and *U-185* were operating along

A US Navy PBM-3 Mariner of VPB-211. Rio de Janeiro can be seen in the background.

The Brazilian Air Force PBY-5 Catalina serialled 01.

the north-east coast; and *U-172* was going south to join *U-199* and *U-513* which were operating close to Rio de Janeiro. Between 21 June and 6 August, a total of 20 ships were attacked and 17 sunk.

In the area near Rio de Janeiro, *U-513* managed to sink four ships and damage one other, but on 19 July it was sunk by US aircraft operating from Florianópolis, as described in the previous chapter. The attacks by this submarine and *U-199*, which sank a ship and damaged another two, led to a reinforcement of operations in the central coastal region of Brazil.

U-199 was launched by the *Kriegsmarine* in November 1942 and left Europe in May 1943 on its first raid, heading south and crossing the Equator on 10 June, arriving at its area of operations on the 18th, which was to the south of 25°S and east of 45°W. After several days without finding enemy ships, it went north towards Rio de Janeiro, and on the 25th was with *U-513* when the latter was attacked by a Fw-58 as described earlier.

According to the crew of *U-199*, on 22 June they sank with gunfire a small sailing ship called *Shangri-La*. Later, on the 24th, they sank the British merchant ship *Henzada* and on 27 June attacked the *Charles W. Peale* with gunfire and torpedoes, to the south of Rio de Janeiro, but the ship survived.

Some days later, on 3 July, an A-28 Hudson took off from Santa Cruz, commanded by Lieutenant Clóvis Labre de Lemos, to cover a convoy travelling north from Santos harbour. At 1100, the crew saw *U-199* 120 miles from their base, in the direction of the island of São Sebastião, where, by the end of the afternoon, the convoy would pass. The submarine immeditately started to dive and an electrical problem prevented the pilot of the Hudson from dropping depth charges, so the plane returned to base. During the afternoon, the Martin Mariner 74-P-6 of VP-74 Squadron, commanded by Lieutenant Harold Carey,

Blimps of the US Navy at Maceió.

A US Navy Blimp operating in Brazil.

was sent to patrol the area, detecting the submarine under the surface. Carey pursued the vessel until nightfall, but while performing an attack at around 2100 the wing of the Mariner hit the water and the plane crashed, killing all of its crew.

The last day of *U-199*

At dawn on 31 July 1943, the PBM-3C Mariner 74-P-7 from VP-74 Squadron, piloted by Lieutenant Walter Smith, took off to protect convoy JT-3, which was departing Rio de Janeiro towards Trinidad. At 0714, radar operator C.R. Wilson detected *U-199* 19 miles from the plane and 70 miles from the entrance to Guanabara Bay. The pilot kept a speed of 120 knots at 4,000ft, and was spotted by the U-Boat when they were 15 miles away, but he only saw it at 10 miles. Smith started to descend and increased his speed to 190 knots. A mile from the target, he levelled the plane at 150ft and a speed of 180 knots, but kept descending slightly to drop the eight Mk-47 depth charges they were carrying from just 75ft. The crew of the submarine opened fire with machine guns and the guns of the vessel, but the pilot managed to aim and drop the charges from 65ft while they were overflying the submarine from the port side, at an angle of 270°. The bomber, Dalton W. Smith, dropped six charges and then the pilot started a new attack, from the bow, at an angle of 350°, dropping the two remaining charges. The tail gunner, J.J. Smith, saw that the bombs of the first attack surrounded the submarine, while the co-pilot, Ensign Claude F. Grotts, saw that the second attack bombs explode very close off the port bow, covering the submarine with water, but as soon as the water column disappeared the crew saw that the submarine was still on the surface and firing its guns. However, the vessel had been damaged and would be an easy target for another attack.

After sailing in circles for a while, the submarine headed north, changing course to face the Mariner when the plane tried to strafe her. At 0804 the submarine tried to dive, but the Mariner crew reported that *U-199* had lost control and was almost sinking. According to the U-Boat's crew, they could dive, but had suffered damage that impeded their ability to sail submerged and they could only continue at a slow speed on the surface. The commander of the submarine decided to approach the coast to dive and put his vessel on the bottom of the ocean to carry out repairs.

Nevertheless, the Mariner had reported the situation and asked for reinforcements. Aspirant-Aviator Sergio Schnoor remembered later that he was at Santos Dumont Airport in Rio de Janeiro when an officer of the US Navy entered the headquarters shouting: 'There is a submarine out there! Go there and get it!' Schnoor was the only pilot there and was sent with the Hudson serialled FAB 73, of the *Unidade Volante do Galeão*, with Captain Almor dos Santos Polycarpo as co-pilot and Sergeants Manuel Gomes de Medeiros Filho and João Antônio Nascimento. As soon as the crew located the position on the map, they took off heading 220°, arriving 20 minutes later over the submarine. *U-199* was still being pursued by the Mariner, which made occasional strafing passes to stop the submarine from diving, while the crew of the submarine were searching for a place to dive, at only 135 metres or less, to make their repairs.

Schnoor recalled:

> When I arrived I saw the PBM; I didn't know of its presence. So I stared at it and thought, 'this comrade is going to attack, let me attack first'. It was taking the bread from his mouth. We manoeuvred and opened the bomb bay. We had already checked the machine guns. We climbed and I was aligned with [the submarine].

At that moment, the crew of the submarine found the right depth to dive, but the Hudson was on its bomb run. Seconds later, the plane attacked *U-199* from the bow and stern, dropping two depth charges from 300ft, which fell 50 metres from the target, but the machine guns hit the submarine, causing some casualties on the deck. On the second pass, they fired again with the machine guns and then returned to base. The PBM kept flying over the submarine, while the Catalina serialled 02 of the FAB, which had also been on a mission to escort convoy JT-3, approached.

This plane was commanded by 2nd Lieutenant Miranda Corrêa, but the commander of the unit, Major Kahl, had ordered Aspirant Alberto Torres, who had more experience, to go along too. Torres remembered:

> On the 31st, at dawn, a convoy of 30 ships was to depart to the north. We, together with two other planes, would sweep the route during the next 24 hours. Other planes would offer direct protection for the convoy. We took off, with Miranda Corrêa making his first solo flight on a Catalina. One hour after take-off, he gave me control of the plane. We flew over the sea parallel to Cabo Frío, heading to the Abrolhos islands. Over Cabo Frío a message gave us the coordinates, 'enemy activity on X sector'; we plotted the position and took that direction. We knew that enemy activity could only be a submarine. We arrived and saw it from far away; we were low, about 1,200 metres, and the weather was good. The vessel was perpendicular to us and we started to descend. When we increased

A US Navy blimp undergoing maintenance in Brazil during the war.

The Lockheed Harpoon, serialled FAB 1156, pictured in the United States in 1945.

A FAB Lockheed Harpoon.

our descent to start our attack, *U-199* turned fast to port, making a 90º turn and aligned with our path, with the bow towards us.

On board the plane were two officers of higher rank as observers, Captain-Aviator José Maria Mendes Coutinho and 1st Lieutenant-Aviator Luiz Gomes Ribeiro. Also aboard were Sergeants Sebastião Domingues, Gelson Abernaz Muniz and Manuel Catarino dos Santos, Corporal Raimundo Henrique Freitas and Private Enísio Silva. When they received the order to go to the combat zone, they were about 50 miles from the submarine.

The Catalina took advantage of the attention the submarine was paying to the Mariner, despite Torres remembering seeing *U-199*'s anti-aircraft artillery firing at them:

The Lockheed Ventura serialled FAB-12, baptized Cavalho Marino.

> I saw an orange blaze from the gun on the nose and because of that I took evasive action before reaching a height of 100 metres, when the plane was stabilized to permit a perfect drop of the bombs. With all the machine guns firing in the last 200 metres, close up with the target we dropped the depth charges over the bow of the submarine. Three Mk-44 depth charges were dropped on the first pass, regulated for a depth of 12 metres, which was the maximum the submarine could dive if they started the manoeuvre at the same moment.

One of the depth charges fell very close to the target, with the others falling further away, but the ship still started to sink. Torres started to turn right for a new attack when Miranda Corrêa, who was operating the button to release the depth charges, saw that, due to the explosion of the charges of the first attack, the ship was almost blown out of the water and immediately halted. On the second pass they dropped a fourth charge over the submarine, but it was seriously damaged by the first charge and was sinking, and the charge fell close to the stern when it was disappearing below the surface. Some crew members managed to jump into the water before, at 0902, the vessel disappeared from view. Of the 61 crew members, 49 were killed and the others were rescued thanks to the Mariner and Catalina crew dropping life rafts to them.

Torres remembered:

> We stayed there, seeing the crew of the submarine we had sunk. A curious thing happened when we dropped the life rafts: they tied them together and started to row. As I speak German, I told them using the Aldis lamp we used to communicate with the convoys 'don't row, there's a ship coming to look for you'. After the first message, nothing happened, but on the second, they stop rowing.

Immediately after, Schnoor arrived back in another Hudson, while a further Mariner also turned up, but with nothing now to do it returned to base. Meanwhile, the hydroplane tender USS *Barnegat* recovered the U-Boat survivors after they had been in the water for two hours. The only survivors were the commander, *Kaptänleutnant* Hans Werner Kraus, aged 28, three officers, four petty officers and four sergeants. As soon as they arrived on land they were put on a *Panair do Brasil* plane and sent to the United States to be interrogated.

On 28 August of that year, the Catalina was baptised with the name *Arará*, which was one of the merchant ships sunk by *U-507* in 1942. The plane, still wearing a US Navy paint scheme, had on its tail the inscription 'Donated to the FAB by the people of Carioca'.

Torres, after flying 64 patrol missions, was sent to the *1º Grupo de Caça* to fly P-47 Thunderbolts in Italy, being the pilot with most combat missions, with more than 100. Miranda Corrêa was also sent to Italy with the same unit.

The Ventura, serialled FAB-7, equipped with rails to fire rockets. Pictured at Fortaleza in August 1944.

A FAB Consolidated PBY-5A Catalina.

The squadron of Venturas at Recife.

Delivery of the PBY-5A Catalina to the FAB.

The Vultee Vengeance had a very short service life in Brazil because of the poor condition in which they arrived in the country.

A Douglas A-20K Havoc of the FAB.

A Vengeance used for ground training.

A Vultee Vengeance of the FAB.

6

OPERATIONS IN BRAZIL UNTIL THE END OF THE WAR

The last attack by the FAB

After the actions during July and other attacks performed by the planes of the US Navy, a total of eight German submarines were sunk near the coast of Brazil between May and September. The German *Kriegsmarine* command were convinced that in this area the task of the submarine would not be an easy one, and operations were reduced considerably, with the sinking of only one merchant ship in August (the *Bagé*), two in September (*Itapagé* and *Cisne Branco*) and the last one of the year being the *Campos* on 23 October, sunk by *U-170*.

On 30 October, the Catalina serialled 01, of the *1° Grupo de Patrulha* of *Base Aérea do Galeão*, took off to escort a convoy, with Captain Dionísio Cerqueira de Taunay as pilot and co-pilot being Lieutenant Schnoor, who remembered:

> We left on a normal mission to protect a convoy. The convoy was sailing close to Cabo Frío and when we arrived we started to fly around it. When we were on the leg heading south of the patrol rectangle, we saw a suspect object far away. Taunay alerted the crew and prepared the bombs, regulating the interval between them with the intervalometer. It was about 10 in the morning. The Catalina kept losing altitude until reaching the ideal height for an attack. The opposition was formidable. They fired with everything they had. We

A Havoc of the FAB.

A Noorduyn Norseman of the FAB.

A FAB Harpoon in the United States.

The Norsemans were widely used by the Correio Aéreo Nacional for air mail duties.

> felt a violent longitudinal vibration when they hit our right engine. We dropped three Mk-47 depth charges, but one of them didn't fall and remained with the plane until we returned. The charges fell close to the target and we saw debris on the sea next to where the charges fell. The result of the attack was considered dubious, as no pictures were taken and nobody witnessed if the vessel sank. The debris could have been launched by the submarine to create confusion and evade new attacks, so was no evidence of a sinking.

Most probably, the submarine was the *U-170* which, after operating in the area, returned to the North Atlantic and survived the war. Schnoor added:

> During the attack dive from 500ft at an angle of about 30 degress, the submarine, using its anti-aircraft weapons, with 107mm and 88mm guns, hit the right engine and the fuselage. The plane was surrounded by red and black coloured explosions, which left a smell of cordite in the cabin and gave us the sensation of a real combat.

A Curtiss P-40 of the FAB.

Sergeants Halley Passos and Humberto Mirabelli, the two mechanics of the Catalina, were slightly wounded by fire from the submarine.

Immediately after, a Hudson commanded by Aspirant Torres took off and passed the Catalina on their return. After an hour on patrol, they saw only an oil stain on the sea.

The *UsBaTu*

The lack of training of Brazilian pilots was evident in the first half of 1943 when in many attacks the planes did not reach their targets. It was agreed by the 4th Squadron of the US Navy on 23 September to create a mixed unit with its personnel and those of the *Força Aérea Brasileira*, with the US personnel providing training on the Lockheed-Vega PV-1 Ventura, a much-improved version of the Hudson. This unit started functioning at Natal on 1 October 1943 and was called United States-Brazilian Training Unit (UsBaTu), under the command of Lieutenant Commander Thomas D. Davies. It was decided that they would only train the personnel of one squadron, which would later be equipped with the model. Each pilot performed at least 100 hours of training, including antisubmarine operations, navigation, use of the radar, convoy protection operations and maritime patrols. All operational procedures were standardised with those of the US Navy, both on the normal operations and security and on operational

A P-40 of the FAB.

Delivery of Venturas for the USBATU on 30 March 1944.

A Lockheed Ventura of the FAB during a patrol flight in 1944.

The first Douglas C-47 of the FAB which, together with the Lodestar, signaled the beginning of the modernization of the transport aviation.

A Lockheed Ventura performing a patrol flight over the sea.

A B-25 of the FAB during the war.

Brazilian Air Force Venturas armed with rockets.

missions, being a major improvement for the FAB.

Crews from VB-143 Squadron (which arrived in Brazil in the second half of the year) were in charge of the training at Recife and São Luis.

Once the training was finished, the personnel were distributed among the US Navy units operating in Brazil to gain experience. Some of those who graduated were sent to Quonset Point Naval Base, near Boston, to improve their training and learn about antisubmarine operations with radar and using the new 127mm HVAR (High Velocity Aircraft Rockets).

Thanks to this course, the FAB started to have crews that were really well-trained for antisubmarine operations. Unfortunately, however, their knowledge could not be put into practice.

Operations of the US Navy

After July, the activity of German submarines increased closer to the African coast, so the VB-107 was transferred to Ascension Island

A P-40 at Canoas.

P-40 planes flying near the Brazilian coast in 1944.

between September and October, but one of their planes, named Gallopin' Ghost, crashed while taking off at Natal on 15 October and, despite the crew escaping, was written off. The VB-107 kept operating on the island and did not return to Brazil.

Shortly after, the last sinking along the Brazilian coast in the war took place. On 23 September, *U-161* was sunk near Bahía, with depth charges launched by a Mariner of VP-74.

After that, the only sinking near the area was that of *U-848* on 5 November, to the south-west of Ascension Island, with depth charges launched by three B-24 Liberators and two B-25 Mitchells of VB-107 and the 1st Compron (Composite Squadron) of the US Army.

Before the end of the year, more changes took place to the squadrons, with the arrival of VB-130 Squadron with 12 PV-1 Venturas at Fortaleza, to replace VB-127. VB-143 also arrived with 12 PV-1 Venturas at Recife, along with VB-145 with 12 PV-1 Venturas at Natal, VP-203 with 12 PBM-3 Mariners at Salvador to replace VP-74, and VP-211 with 12 PBM-3 Mariners at Rio de Janeiro.

Fleet Airship Wing 4 also arrived in September 1943 with blimp squadrons ZP-41 and ZP-42, equipped with K-Class blimps, to carry out ASW (antisubmarine warfare) and SAR (search and rescue) operations, but they had no contact with enemy submarines.

In April 1944, VP-45 arrived with PBY-5A Catalinas and was deployed at Salvador, while VB-130 and VB-143 returned to the United States.

In October, unit names were changed, all becoming VPB- and keeping their number. Besides the main FAB bases, the planes operated regularly from Amapá, Igarap-e-Açú, São Luis, Maceió, Fernando de Noronha, Caravelas and Vitória.

During 1944, American forces only sank *U-177* on 6 February, to the west of Ascension Island, at the hands of a Liberator of VB-107. On 28 September, *U-863* was found near Recife by the Liberator 107-B-4 of VP-211, but intense fire from the submarine led the crew to abort the attack. Informed of the position, two Liberators (107-B-7 and 107-B-9) of VB-107 searched for the vessel on the following day and found her. The plane serialled 107-B-9, under command of Lieutenant John Burton, made the first attack and damaged the *U-863* extensively, preventing her from submerging. Shortly after, 107-B-7 performed three attacks and destroyed the submarine. Despite around 20 men being seen in the water and life rafts being dropped, they were never found.

In the meantime, in August 1944 the VP-94 sent a detachment of five Catalinas commanded by Lieutenant Commander Richard Craig to Santa Cruz Air Base in Rio de Janeiro to support the training of the Brazilian Catalina crews in ASW tactics. Each group was trained there for one month and then the first group, trained from 15 August, went to Salvador for two months to keep training there on operational sorties with VPB-45 which arrived equipped with PBY-5A Catalinas.

US Navy units operated until the end of the war, but there were no more attacks against German submarines.

New planes for the FAB

During 1943, deliveries of materiel from the United States continued, including 20 P-40Ks, 76 AT-6 Texans, 63 Fairchild PT-19s, 57 Vultee BT-15s, 20 UC-78s, five Lockheed Lodestars and many examples of Beechcraft AT-7s, AT-11s and C-45s. As can be seen, the main effort was in expanding training capacity, but in 1944 this changed considerably, as the quantity of aircraft delivered was reduced to 10 Beech D-17Ss, 12 Norsemans, 13 BT-15s, nine C-45s and AT-7s, six AT-6 Texans, one UC-78 and the first four Douglas C-47s. Between August and November of that year, 21 North American B-25J Mitchells arrived, and in July 30 Douglas A-20K Havocs. The Havocs were initially sent to Santa Cruz for training, to be sent later to operational units.

In the meantime, on 30 March the UsBaTu was considered finished and on that day 14 Lockheed PV-1 Venturas were delivered to the graduated crews, and planes and personnel formed the *1º Grupo de Bombardeio Medio* (*1º GBM*), also known as *1º Grupo de Venturas*. This unit replaced VB-143 Squadron of the US Navy at Recife, with responsibility to protect convoys in the area between João Pessoa and the mouth of the São Francisco River, having under their control the blimp squadron of the US Navy.

In April, four Lockheed PV-2 Harpoons joined the force and went to Salvador Air Base, while their crews were trained by personnel of *1º GBM*.

With the new training and the arrival of new planes, the Brazilians progressively replaced US units, which started to return to their home country.

During 1944, the United States also delivered 28 Vultee V-72s/A-31 Vengeances and five A-35Bs to create two dive bomber units.

Meanwhile, during the year only two ships were sunk by submarines near Brazil, starting with the transport *Vital de Oliveira*, of the Brazilian Navy, on the night of 19-20 July, torpedoed by *U-861*. The destroyer *Javari*, which was escorting the ship, tried unsuccessfully

An A-20 Havoc of the FAB.

A-20 Havocs were the main attack planes of the FAB during the war years where they replaced the Vultee V-11s.

A-20 Havocs of the FAB.

to chase the submarine. Shortly after, on the 21st, the *Camaquã* was sunk, supposedly by the same submarine. After that, no more activity of German or Italian submarines was detected along the Brazilian coast.

Shortly before that, on 2 July, the deployment of the *Força Expedicionária Brasileira* (FEB), which would fight in Italy together with Allied forces, began. On that day, the first forces departed Rio de Janeiro on the transport USS *General Mann*, escorted by three destroyers. On 22 September, the same transport started a second trip, together with the USS *General Meighs*, with two cruisers and two destroyers as escort.

On 23 November, another group departed on the USS *General Meighs*, and on 8 February 1945, the last group left on the same ship. To protect them, a major effort was made by the entire patrol aviation, as on each trip a large number of troops were being carried and a submarine attack on the ships would be a terrible loss. In this effort, the *1º GMB* had the responsibility to make night patrols, thanks to their knowledge of operations with radar and having the most advanced antisubmarine planes in Brazil.

New structure

Until summer 1944, the FAB had experienced an exponential growth, but in a way that was disorganised with regard to air units, keeping a big part of the organisation inherited from the Army and Navy. To improve the organisation, on 17 August 1944, Decree-Law 6796 was issued, modified on 5 October of that year by Decree-Law 6926, changing the organisation of the Air Force, which became as follows:

1º Zona Aérea:
1º Grupo de Patrulha (*1º GpPat*, Patrol Group) at Belém, with PBY Catalinas.
2º Zona Aérea:
1º Grupo Misto de Aviação (*1º GMA*, Aviation Joint Group) at Natal, with B-25 Mitchells and Curtiss P-40E/K-10/K-15/Ms.
2º Grupo de Bombardeio Medio (*2º GpBM*, Medium Bombing Group) at Salvador, with Lockheed PV-2 Harpoons.
4º Grupo de Bombardeio Medio (*4º GpBM*) at Fortaleza, with Lockheed A-28 Hudsons and B-25 Mitchells.
6º Regimento de Aviação at Recife:
1º Grupo de Bombardeio Medio (*1º GpBM*), with Lockheed PV-1 Venturas.
A second group was planned to be created in the near future.
3º Zona Aérea:
1º Grupo de Transporte (*1º GT*, Transport Group) at Aeroporto Santos Dumont, Río de Janeiro, subordinadted to the *Gabinete do Ministro da Aeronáutica* (Aeronautics Ministry Staff), with Douglas C-47s and Lockheed Lodestars.
2º Grupo de Transporte (*2º GT*) at Galeão, Río de Janeiro, subordinated to the *Diretoria de Rotas Aéreas* (Air Routes Directory), with Douglas C-47s.
1º Regimento de Aviação at Santa Cruz:
1º Grupo de Bombardeio Picado (*1º GpBP*, Dive Bombing Group), with Vultee A-31/A-35 Vengeances.
2º Grupo de Caça (*2º GpCa*, Fighter Group), with Curtiss P-40Es/K-10s/K-15s/Ms.
They also had the last Vultee V-11s in service.
4º Regimento de Aviação at Galeão:
3º Grupo de Bombardeio Medio (*3º GpBM*), with Lockheed A-28 Hudsons and B-25 Mitchells.
2º Grupo de Patrulha (*2º GpPat*, Patrol Group), with Consolidated PBY-5 Catalinas.
Escola de Aviação (Aviation School), at Campo dos Afonsos, with Vultee BT-15s, Fairchild PT-19s, Beech C-18Ss, AT-6 Texans, the remaining Fw-44Js, Stearmans and Muniz M-9s and other models.
4º Zona Aérea:
2º Regimento de Aviação at Cumbica, São Paulo:
2º Grupo de Bombardeio Leve (*2º GpBL*, Light Bombing Group) at Cumbica, with Douglas A-20 Havocs.
2º Grupo de Bombardeio Picado (*2º GpBP*) at Cumbica, with Vultee A-31/A-35 Vengeances.
1º Grupo Misto de Instrução (*1º GMI*, Instruction Joint Group), with Douglas B-18 Bolos, one Republic RP-47B Thunderbolt, two B-25s, two P-40s, one A-20 Boston III, one A-35 Vengeance and one Consolidated B-24 Liberator, for ground training.

The Havocs arrived close to the end of the war and took almost no part in patrol missions.

None of them was operational.

5º Zona Aérea:

5º Regimento de Aviação:

1º Grupo de Caça (1º GpCa) at Curitiba (despite being created on paper to operate there, it was officially created in Panama as 1º *Grupo de Aviação de Caça (1º GAvCa)*.

3º Grupo de Bombardeio Picado (1º GpBP) at Curitiba, with Vultee A-31/A-35 Vengeances.

3º Regimento de Aviação:

1º Grupo de Bombardeio Leve (1º GpBL) at Canoas, with Douglas A-20 Havocs. It was used for training with USAAF personnel and disbanded in 1946, with its personnel and equipment sent to the *2º GpBL*.

3º Grupo de Caça (3º GpCa) at Canoas, with Curtiss P-40Es/K-10s/K-15s/Ms.

1º Esquadrilha de Ligação e Observação (1º ELO) at Pisa, Italy, with Piper L-4H Cubs.

Other planes, like the Focke Wulf 58B *Weihe*, Grumman G-44 Widgeon, Beech D-17, liaison planes and many AT-6 Texans, were distributed to different air bases. The Vultee Vengeance had a very short life with the FAB, being retired in 1948.

Despite some German submarines, mainly en route to the Pacific Ocean or Japan, passing nearby there were no further contacts before the end of the war. This situation led to a reduction of US Navy air units in Brazil: by the beginning of 1945, only the Blimp Squadron remained at Maceió, the others having returned to the United States. Despite there being plans to transfer the blimps to the FAB and for personnel of the force to receive training on their operation in the United States, this was later discarded. During the war, none of the blimps based in Brazil had any contact with enemy vessels. Meanwhile, in December 1944, 15 PBY-5A Catalinas were received, increasing further the capacity for maritime patrols.

Havocs flying in formation. They were based at São Paulo.

The 2º *GAvCa*

With the new organization, the *2º Grupo de Caça (2º GpCa)* was created under the command of Colonel Ismar Brasil, and later named *2º GAvCa*, equipped with P-40N Warhawks, which were the most modern figthers in Brazil. While the unit was being organized in Brazil with pilots and mechanics, a group of 33 pilots and mechanics were sent to Panama for training, commanded by Captain Ildeu da Cunha Pereira; they returned to Brazil to keep operational training with their own planes at Santa Cruz, under the guidance of USAAF Colonel Norval C. Bonawitz, who was in charge of their preparation. The original plan was to deploy them to Europe, but the end of the war in that theatre led to the cancellation of such plans. When, on 6 June 1945, Brazil declared war on Japan, it was rumoured the unit would be sent as the *2º GAvCa* to the Pacific theatre, so the pilots continued their training. During operations, Aspirante Sá de Osório was killed in an accident when his P-40N FAB 4061 hit the towed target during a firing practice.

Eventually, as the war finished before their training was complete, they were never deployed.

By the end of the Second World War, the *Força Aérea Brasileira* was the most powerful and experienced in Latin America, with a huge knowledge of antisubmarine operations, together with a large number of fighter, attack and transport aircraft.

PART 3: OPERATIONS IN ITALY

7

THE 1º ELO

When it was decided to send units to Italy it was considered that, besides sending a fighter unit, it was important to also have an observation unit. This would support the *Força Expedicionária Brasileira* (FEB) – that would fight on the ground in the Mediterranean theatre – by adjusting artillery fire. When the deployment of this force was originally conceived, the plan was that they would fight in North Africa, but the defeat of the Germans in Tunisia and the invasion of the Italian peninsula determined they would end fighting in Italy.

Accordingly, on 20 July 1944, by Ministerial Advice 57, Minister of Aeronautics Salgado Filho created the *1º Esquadrilha de Ligação e Observação (1º ELO)*. Besides performing liaison and reconnaissance missions this would also support the *Artilharía Divisionaria (AD,*

A Piper of the 1º ELO over the Apennines. (Author's collection)

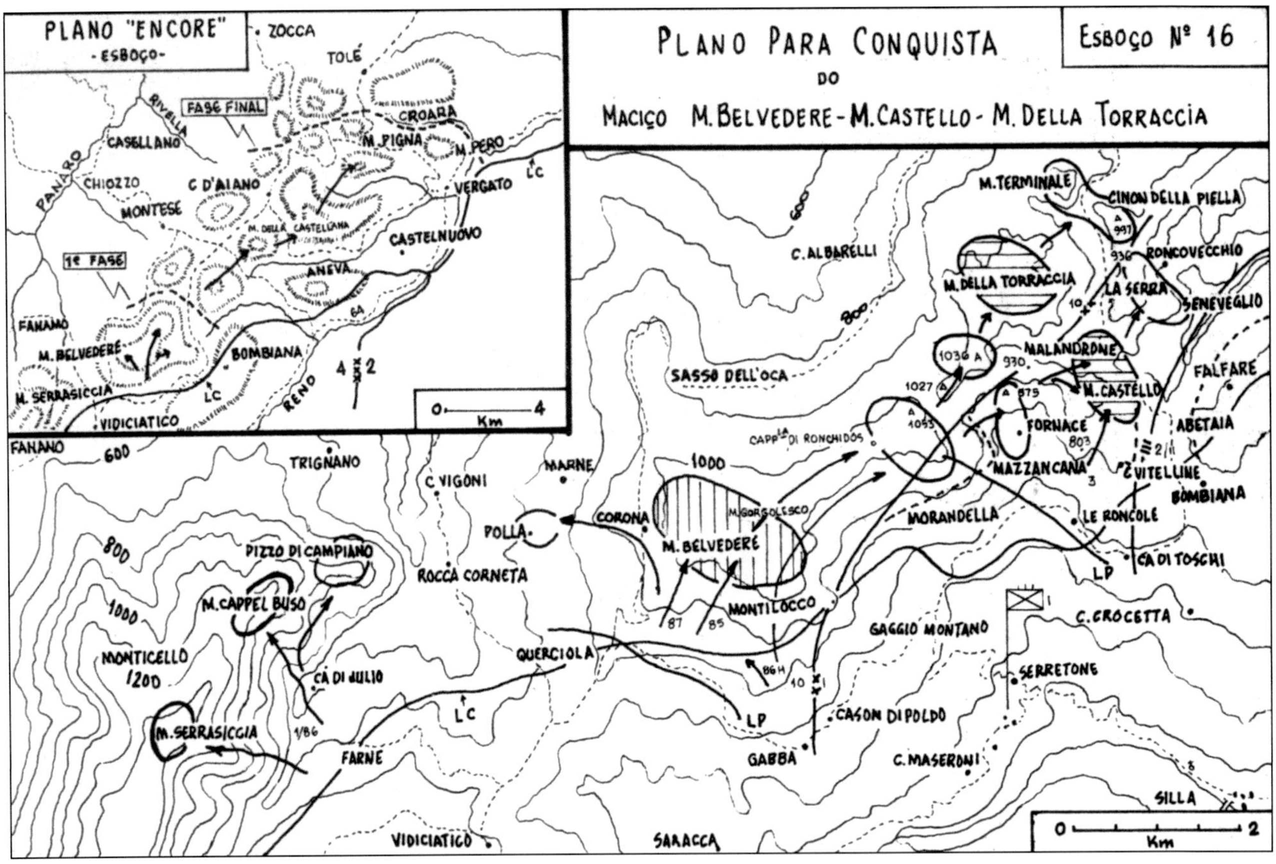

Map of Operation Encore. (Author's collection)

Artillery Division) of the *1º Divisão de Infantaria* (Infantry Division) of the FEB. Eleven days after its creation, Captain João Affonso Fabrício Belloc was appointed as its commander (and promoted to major in Italy), and was assigned 10 pilot officers, another officer for administrative work, eight mechanic sergeants, two radio specialist sergeants and eight mechanic soldiers.

The unit would operate the Piper L-4H, named Teco-Teco by the Brazilians, with 65hp Continental engines and equipped with radio but without armament, which would be delivered in Italy from the USAAF stocks. The model had not been used by the FAB, so training was performed at *Campo dos Afonsos* on Fairchild PT-19 planes, which were not the best suited to prepare the crews for such missions. The end of their 40 days of training featured a demonstration of the Divisional Artillery, with the adjustments made by the *1º ELO*, and on 19 September the personnel of the unit presented at the *1º Regimento de Obuses Auto-Rebocado* (1st Regiment of Towed Howitzers) at Rio de Janeiro, to wait for their transport to the Mediterranean. Three days later, they departed on board the USS *General Meighs*.

The unit arrived at Naples on 6 October 1944 with the second group of the FEB, and on the 10th was transferred to Livorno on landing vessel LC-1-116, arriving two days later. From there they moved to San Giusto Aerodrome in Pisa, where they received the 10 planes they

Douglas A-20K Havoc – Thirty Douglas A-20K Havocs were delivered and used for attack purposes at Cumbica, São Paulo and Canoas, Río Grande do Sul. They performed patrol missions during the war but saw no action. The plane with constructor number 6085 had the USAF serial number 44-539 and FAB serial number FAB 25 later becoming FAB 6085. Currently it is the only surviving Havoc in Brazil.

Douglas B-18 Bolo – Three Bolos were the first US-built twin-engined bombers of the force and used during the first stage of anti-submarine operations, damaging U-154 on 8 May 1943. By then they were serving at the Grupo de Aviões Bimotores at Recife and Natal. The plane 37-032 became FAB serial number 5027 and was retired in 1949.

North American B-25B Mitchell – Together with the Bolos, a batch of six B-25Bs was received in January 1942, followed by another one for ground training. They took part on the first ASW operations against Axis submarines. The 40-2310 was later serialled FAB-06 and then FAB 5033 and retired in 1949. They served at the Grupo de Aviões Bimotores at Recife and Natal in 1943.

Focke Wulf Fw-58 Weihe – The Weihe 2-V-4 of the Brazilian Navy was received in 1938 and transferred to the FAB in 1941. On 25 June 1943 an unidentified Weihe performed the only attack by this model against a German submarine.

Curtiss P-40E – Six P-40Es were delivered with the first batch of fighters in 1942, serving at the Grupo Monoposto Monomotor, together with the P-36. They were later joined by nine P-40Ks. They wore colours received in the US, with the Brazilian markings applied.

Republic P-47D Thunderbolt serial 42-29265, received in Italy in February 1945 – This plane was pressed into service with the FAB in Brazil in 1946 but grounded in 1947 and used for spares. A few Thunderbolts used by the Brazilians had the metal finish scheme.

Republic P-47D Thunderbolt serial 42-26786, used in Italy from October 1944 – Damaged on missions 268, 389 and 430 and later sent to Brazil and assigned to 2º Grupo de Caça on 7-1-46. Later transferred to 1º/4º GAv on 10-1-57 and lost in an accident on 17-12-57 while being ferried to PqAerSP. The plane seen here is without the dorsal fin installed shortly after the arrival of the Brazilians to Italy.

Consolidated PBY-5 Catalina serialled 02 and named "Arará" after sinking the U-199 – After the U-199 was damaged by a US Navy Martin Mariner and a FAB Hudson on 31 July 1943, the vessel was sunk by the Catalina, the only confirmed kill by the Brazilians in the ASW war along their coast. The Catalina was named after one of the sunken Brazilian merchant ships which belonged to the Unidade Volante do Galeão.

Piper L-4H of the 1º ELO – Apart from the 1º GAvCa, the Força Expedicionaria Brasileira had the 1º ELO as their air units, with the last performing spotting missions to guide the ground artillery. They moved constantly from airfield to airfield while the frontline was progressing to the north of Italy.

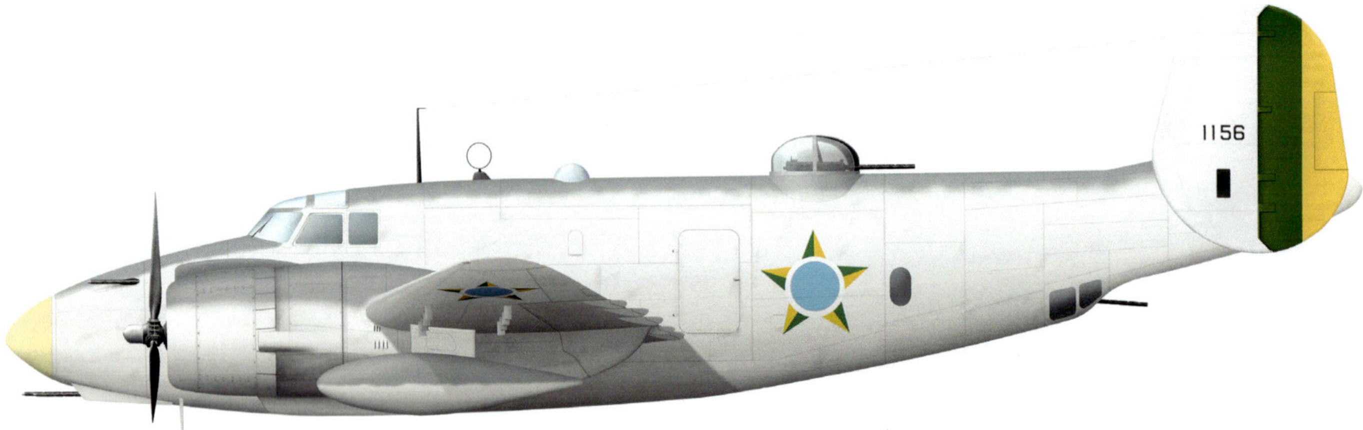

Lockheed PV-2 Harpoon – with the serial FAB 1156 used before delivery. This serial wasn't used in Brazil. Six Harpoons were delivered to the FAB in April 1945 to increase the fleet of Hudsons and Venturas, serving at the 2º Grupo de Bombardeio Medio.

Vultee V-11 – Twenty-six Vultee V-11s were acquired by the Brazilian Army shortly before the war and 24 were transferred to the FAB in 1941. In August 1942 the plane serialled 122 attacked a submarine but they couldn't verify if they caused damage.

The plane of the profile belonged to the 1º Regimento de Aviação of the Army, in 1940.

Badge of 1º ELO. (Author's collection)

Badge of the 1st GAvCa. (Author's collection)

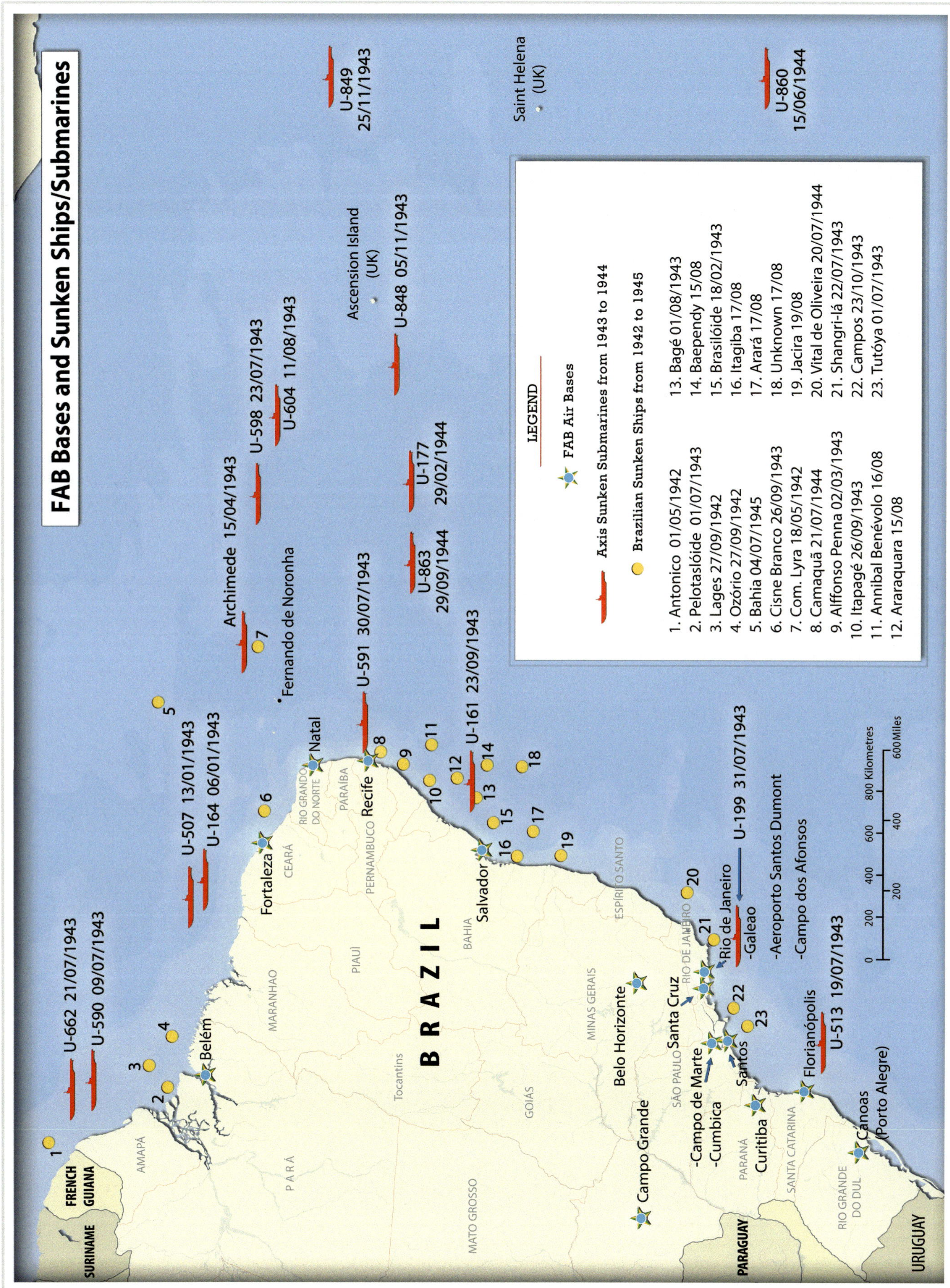

FAB Bases, sunken ships and submarines.

Italian Operations Theatre.

Crews and Brazilian nurses with the Desert Lil. This plane belonged to the USAAF but was delivered to the Brazilians. It was used on liaison duties until it had an accident while landing and was written off in 1945. (John Buyers)

Crews at Pisa. In the background the destroyed hangars can be seen. The base was almost completely destroyed by bombing before being captured by Allied forces. No hangars were left for the maintenance of the Brazilian fighters. (John Buyers)

Lara de Araujo in March, 1945, on the wing of his plane. (John Buyers)

Mechanics posing to the camera on a P-47D. (John Buyers)

Planes of 1º ELO deployed in Italy. (Author's collection)

A Piper L-4H of 1º ELO landing on an Italian airfield. (Author's collection)

would operate. Eight of them received the names '*Grupo Escola*', '*Brasil*', '*Bandeirante*', '*Santa Therezinha*', '*Timbiras*', '*Ceará*', '*Diogo Júnior*' and '*Luly*', and were painted with USAAF colours, but they later received yellow and green stripes on the tail and the Brazilian colours painted over those of the USAAF. From San Giusto, where they were adapted to the model and started their training, on 4 November they moved to start operations from San Rossore hippodrome at Pisa, occupied by the British and transformed into an aerodrome.

Their missions were difficult, because it was the beginning of winter, with low temperatures that the Brazilians were not accustomed to, and they were flying over the Apennines on lengthy missions, facing enemy fire.

Because of the movements of the FEB, especially the *Cuartel General de la Artilharia Divisionaria* (Divisional Artillery Headquarters), the *1º ELO* regularly had to change their base, which in many cases were only small grass or dust strips, 200-300 metres in length and with very few facilities.

On 12 November, 1st Lieutenant Aviator João Torres Leite Soares and observer Army 1st Lieutenant Oswaldo Mescolin flew on the plane serialled 1-4H-5 on the first operational mission, over the Reno Valley, supporting the FEB, which was preparing to secure road 64, the line of communications and supply for the conquest of Bologna.

On the following day, they moved to San Giorgio aerodrome at Pistóia, 50km to the north-east of Pisa, from where on 17 November they performed several operational missions. Between 26 November and 12 December, they operated daily, adjusting the artillery fire on a front 15km wide, while they monitored the movements of the 232nd and 362nd Divisions of the German Army, which were facing the FEB forces.

Because of the progress of the ground forces, which were nearing the northern end of the Apennines, on 12 December they were ordered to deploy to a small strip on the shores of Lake Suviana, 25km north-east of Pistóia and on the other side of the main range of the Apennines. They were only 6km from the FEB headquarters with its commander, General Mascarenhas de Moraes, at Porretta Terme.

From there, they began actions against the area of Mounts Belvedere, Castello and Della Torracia, which were part of the Gothic Line, the last German defensive line to the south of the Po River valley. The ground troops encountered fierce opposition at Monte Castello, from where they protected the route to Bologna, which was unsuccessfully attacked by the US Army on 24 November and by Brazilian units on 29 November and 5 December.

During the winter, the front line was static, but combat and harassment continued, forcing the *1º ELO* to operate constantly despite the cold and snow. Night missions were then attempted, but they were not possible because of a lack of instruments to fly in mountainous terrain and in bad weather. These planes helped to locate many German units when they were moving, including artillery and infantry units, and to attack them with FEB artillery.

Personnel of 1º ELO in front of their planes. (Author's collection)

At 0600 on 20 February 1945, the three infantry regiments that formed the FEB (the 1st, 6th and 11th) began their advance over Monte Castello, while the 10th Mountain Division of the US Army occupied Monte Della Torracia, which dominated one of the flanks. These were the opening moves of Operation Encore, which included the capture of Mount Belvedere. During the fierce battle that occurred during this day, Piper L-4s of the *1º ELO* guided the artillery, while the first mission of the day by the P-47s of the *1º GAvCa* destroyed a German artillery position on Mount Belvedere.

At 1730, Brazilian forces occupied the top of the mountain while the Americans were still fighting on the Della Torracia. This attack was also preceded by a heavy artillery barrage, guided by the planes of *1º ELO*.

After these actions, it was decided that the *1º ELO* should operate from a strip built using aluminium plates at Porreta Terme, while they awaited the beginning of the spring offensive. The FEB was to advance to the north-west, towards the border with France.

Once the offenseive started on 14 April, the squadron took part in the conquest of Montese, 3.5km to the north of Monte Della Torracia, followed by the advance over Montebufone-Montello on the next two days and the capture of Zocca on the 21st. The troops kept advancing over Route 623, entering the Po Valley and occupying the city of Vignola on 22 April.

The advance continued to the north-west, parallel to the Apennines, but across the Po Valley. The *1º ELO* therefore moved to Montecchio Emilia, only 15km from the centre of Parma, on 27 April. As the German troops retreated faster, the changes of base became more frequent and over longer distances. On 4 May, the unit moved to Piacenza, over the Po River and 70km from the former base. On 9 May, they continued to Portalbera, 30km to the west of Piacenza, following the Po River, where they stayed until the end of the war. Despite the advance of the troops continuing, the speed of the German retreat took them well away from Brazilian forces, and on 29 April the *1º ELO* had performed its last combat sortie. This involved the plane serialled 1-4H-6, commanded by Aspirant Aviator Cornelio Lopes Cançado, with Army 2nd Lieutenant Iônio Portela Ferreira Alves as observer.

Later, on 12 June, they received orders to move to Bergamo, and two days later the following was published in the *Boletim Interno* (Internal Bulletin) nº 73-A of the *Artilharia Divisionária do Exército*, in the theatre of operations:

> According to the verbal order from Division General, Commander of the *1º DIE* (Expeditionary Division), the *Esquadrilha de Ligação e Observação* is extinct. Because of this, its personnel should join up with the *1º Grupo de Aviação de Caça* of the FAB at Pisa.

During some missions, the crews carried hand grenades to drop on the German troops, but without causing any other than a psychological effect. During winter, it was common that ice formed on the carburettor of their aircraft, stopping the engine, and the pilot would glide until reaching a lower altitude and the ice melted, so he could start the engine again.

The badge of the unit was made by Captain Fortunato Câmara de Oliveira of the *1º GAvCa*, at the request of the commander of the *1º ELO*.

In total, the *1º ELO* recorded 2,388 flying hours in Italy on 1,956 flights, of which 1,282 were combat missions, accomplishing 684 missions in 184 days of operations, performing 400 artillery adjustment missions for Brazilian, American and British troops without losing any aircraft. They usually flew with observers from the Brazilian Army, but also flew with four from the British Army (who did 22 missions) and a Brazilian war correspondent.

8
THE 1º GRUPO DE AVIAÇÃO DE CAÇA

On 18 December 1943, Decree No. 6123 created the *1º Grupo de Aviação de Caça* (*1º GavCa*, 1st Fighter Group), which was the unit to be sent to the Mediterranean, while on the 27th of the month, Major Nero Moura was named as its commander. He would select the more important men for the unit, with the remaining ones being volunteers. Among the latter were some who had some experience on the P-40, while others had flown with the Hudsons and Catalinas recently delivered to the FAB, fighting against German submarines. Among them was 2nd Lieutenant Aviator Alberto Martins Torres and 1st Lieutenant Aviator José C. de Miranda Corrêa, both crew members of the Catalina that on 31 July sunk the German submarine *U-199*, the only confirmed submarine sinking by the Brazilians. In total, the team comprised 76 officers - pilots and ground personnel - plus about 300 petty officers and soldiers.

With the aim of the Brazilians learning the way US Army Air Force (USAAF) units operate, to which they would be subordinated, it was decided to send them to USAAF units for intensive training. Because of this, in January 1944, the 32 main officers - called Key Men - started their training in Orlando, Florida, at the USAAF School of Applied Tactics, moving to the nearby Alachua Army Air Field at Gainesville, where they flew P-40Ns until 10 March. Meanwhile, in February the pilots who had no experience on the P-40 were trained on the model at Natal and Recife air bases. After that, the personnel were transferred to Albrook Field, in the Panama Canal Zone, where they were taken to Aguadulce aerodrome, base of the 30th Fighter Squadron of the USAAF, equipped with two RP-40Bs, 22 RP-40Cs, 17 RP-40Es and P-40Ns, besides some AT-6D Texans, North American BC-1s and Vultee BT-13As, under the command of Colonel Gabriel P. Disosway.

Because training was progressing fast, on 11 March 1944 the *1º GAvCa* received the mission to take part in the defence of the Panama Canal Zone, together with US units and using USAAF planes, keeping four squadrons on constant alert.

On 18 May, during one of the training flights, the first loss of the

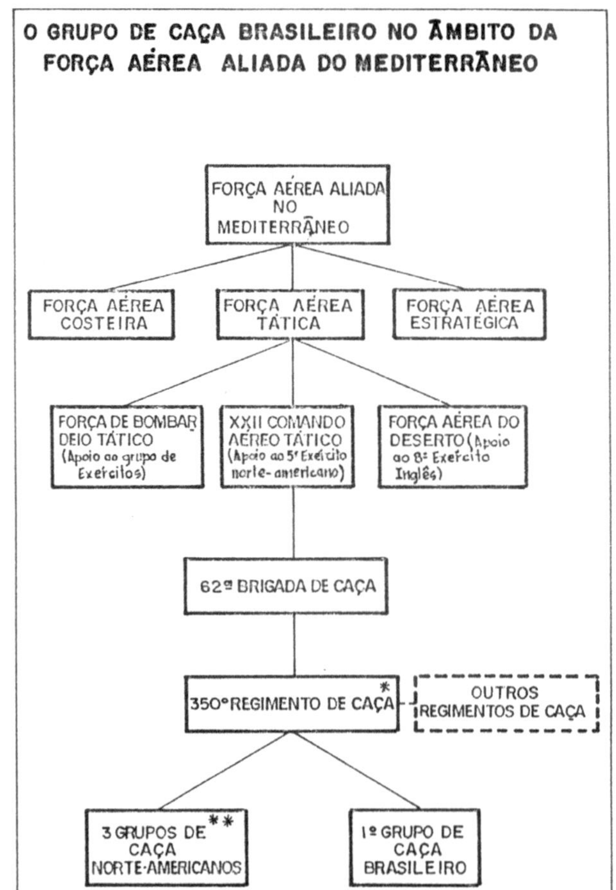

Fonte: Nelson Freire Lavenère-Wanderley, História da Força Aérea Brasileira

Organization of the Mediterranean Allied Air Forces. (Author's collection)

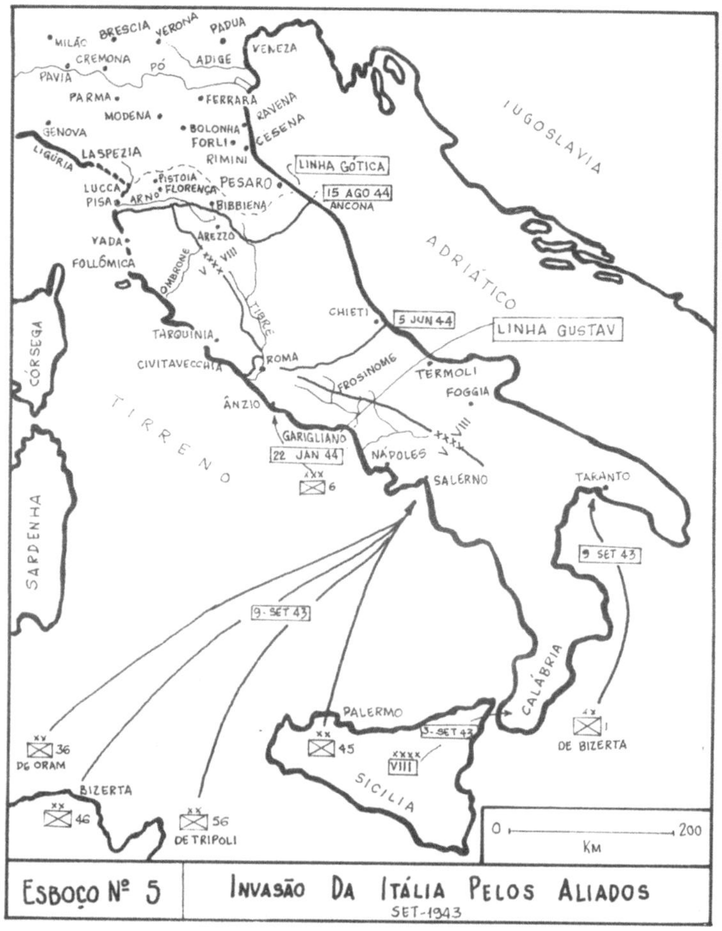

The Italian theatre by September 1943. (Author's collection)

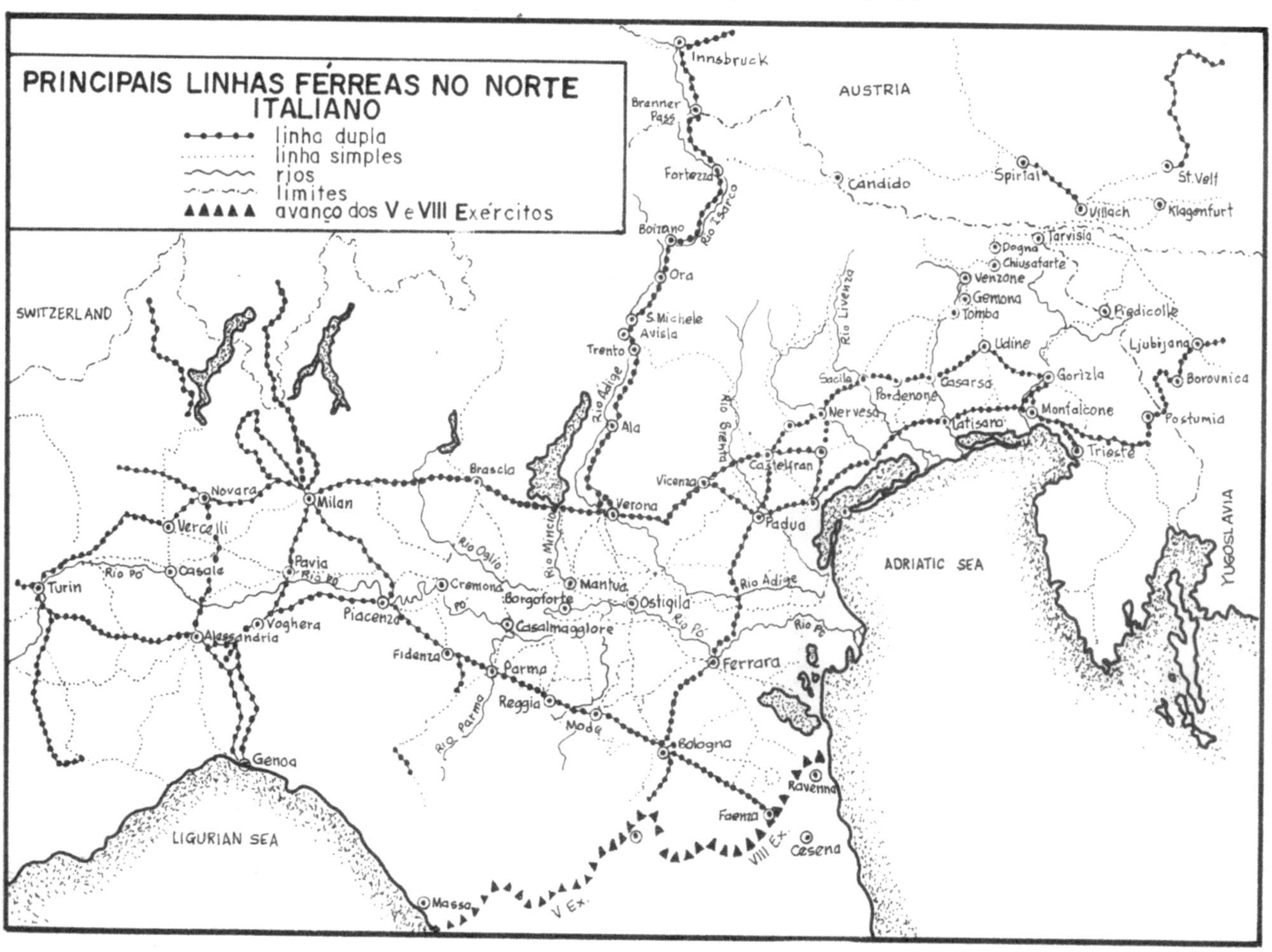

Main railways in northern Italy. (Author's collection)

From left to right: Goulart, Cox, 'Joel Brown', Medeiros and Meira. (Author's collection)

From left to right: Miranda Corrêa, Torres, Pamplona and an unknown man with a Curtiss RP-40B in Panama. (Author's collection)

From left to right: Neiva, Lafayette, a USAF captain, Lagares, Pamplona and Gibson. (Author's collection)

unit took place, when 2nd Lieutenent Dante I. Gastaldoni crashed into the ground when he could not recover from a dive during a combat training mission.

Later, on 22 June and after 110 hours of flight for each pilot, they finished their training. However, some were considered as not qualified for combat and returned to Brazil, while others were trained as radar operators and sent to Italy. Some, though, did make it to fly missions with the group during the war.

From the Panama Canal, they went by ship to New York, where they arrived on 4 July, and from there they went to the Suffolk County Army Air Field, base of the 132nd Army Air Field Base Unit (Fighter), equipped with 34 Republic P-47Cs and four P-47D Thunderbolts. There they learned how to use the model they would use in Italy, where they would be taken, and seven pilots arrived from Brazil, four of them with much experience in Brazil and the others having performed the adaptation course to the Thunderbolt with the P-47 Replacement Unit at Harding Army Air Field in Louisiana. The P-47 was selected in place of the P-38 Lightning and P-51D Mustang.

Meanwhile, the first force of 5,000 men of the *Força Expedicionária Brasileira* (FEB) was travelling to Italy, while the *Esquadrilha de Ligação e Observação* (*1º ELO*, Observation and Liaison Squadron) was created to participate in Italy supporting the FEB artillery units, using Piper Cubs.

Despite it being planned that each pilot should have 93 flying hours before being deployed to the front line, the lack of planes and the skill of the FAB pilots led to the decision on 31 August to finish the training when most had reached only 70 hours. During their training, they performed several combat training sorties against the Grumman F6F Hellcats and Vought F4U Corsairs of the US Navy based at Naval Air Station (NAS) Bridgeport.

9
TARQUÍNIA

On 19 September, the Brazilians boarded the US transport UST *Colombie*, in which they crossed the Atlantic Ocean as part of a convoy and entered the Mediterranean Sea, arriving on 6 October, after a stop in Naples, at the Italian harbour of Livorno, where they disembarked. They immediately went to the aerodrome of the city of Tarquínia, 96km to the north-west of Rome, where the *Reggia Aeronautica* and *Luftwaffe* operated in the past and which was now the base of the 350th Fighter Group of the USAF, to which the *1º GAvCa* would be subordinated, being the fourth squadron of the unit. The group was also subordinated to the 62nd Fighter Wing of the 12th Air Force, and was formed by the 345th 'Devil Hawk', 346th 'Checkerboard' and 347th 'Screaming Red Ass' squadrons, who had recently replaced their

Lafayette on board a 30th Fighter Squadron P-40E. (Author's collection)

Line up of the 30th Fighter Squadron at Panama. (Author's collection)

The only RP-47E delivered to Brazil. (Author's collection)

A P-47D of the 132nd Army Air Field Base Unit (Fighter) during training in the USA. (Author's collection)

P-39 Airacobra for the P-47D Thunderbolt. Also on the small base were another Fighter Group of the USAAF and a RAF Fighter Wing.

The base had only very precarious installations, because it had been heavily bombed, had no hangars and only a part of the concrete runway was in good conditions, while all personnel were living in tents. The mud generated by the rain caused many problems, and in some cases the planes had to be towed to the runway, which was named Runway Island because it was the only place in the aerodrome which was not full of mud. 1st Lieutenant Rui Moreira Lima remembers that:

> The Americans had three Fighter Groups in the Mediterranean theatre equipped with P-47s, the 27th, the 56th and the 350th. The missions for those groups came from the rear, from the headquarters at Caserta, close to Naples. Each group had three squadrons and ours had four, because of the Brazilian squadron.

The Brazilian group was divided into four escadrilles: *Azul* (Blue), *Verde* (Green), *Vermelha* (Red) and *Amarela* (Yellow) with the codes A, B, C and D respectively, followed by the number of each plane. Major Moura and the Operations Officer, Major Oswaldo Pamplona Pinto, were not part of any squadron, and their planes had the number 1 and 2 respectively. Unlike the USAAF planes, the first 31 planes delivered to the Brazilians were painted in olive drab on the upper part and light blue on the lower one, except those of Moura and Pamplona,

1º Tenente Aviador João Eduardo Magalhães Motta on board the RP-47B on 15 December 1944. (Author's collection)

The only RP-47B, serial 41-6037. (Author's collection)

Aerial view of the San Jiusto airfield in Pisa. (Author's collection)

A Thunderbolt armed with bombs is refuelled for a mission. (Author's collection)

which were in polished metal. The Brazilian ensign was applied by modifying the US one, changing the colours of the star and applying a green and a yellow stripe on the rudder. The US serials were kept and the badge of the unit, created by Captain Fortunato Câmara de Oliveira, with the battle-cry '*Senta a Pua*', which means to run against the enemy with decision, to annihilate him.

Once they were installed at the base, the P-47Ds began to be delivered: in total 68 were assigned to them, but many remained in storage at the Army Air Force Storage Center/ Mediterranean Theatre of Operations (AAFSC/MTO) at Capodichino, Naples, to replace losses. Twenty of them would finally be used by USAAF squadrons, delivered with Brazilian colours. In total, the *1º GAvCa* used 48 planes of the models P-47D-25-RE, P-47D-27-RE, P-47D-28-RA, P-47D-28-RE and P-48D-30-RE. Most of the planes delivered were of the model 25-RE, together with some 27-RE and 28-RA, which were different from the others by having a Curtiss Electric AI 14 propeller instead of the Hamilton Standard Hydromatic 24E50.

On 14 October, the first tests flights took place to familiarise the pilots with the area, while the training continued, including bombing and strafing missions with live weapons.

Despite it initially being planned that the main mission for the

From left to right: Meira, Assis and Moreira Lima listen to instructions from Lagares before a mission of the Green Escadrille. (Author's collection)

A rare propaganda shot, taken in the United States, with a purpose-painted plane in Brazilian colours flying together with a British one. The Brazilian plane was finally delivered to the USAAF. (Author's collection)

Ready for a mission. (Author's collection)

The plane 42-26784 was shot down on mission 324 on 9 April 1945. (Author's collection)

Sergeant Robson Saldanha with the Senta a Púa badge. (Author's collection)

Brazilians would be to escort Allied bombers on their route to Germany, the almost complete control of air space in the zone led to the decision to use them on bombing, interdiction and armed reconnaissance missions in support of the Fifth Army of the United States, to which the FEB was dependant, and of the Eighth British Army. Because of this, their main targets were railroads, bridges, vehicles, storage and other enemy facilities. By then, the Allied advance was reaching the northern part of the Apennines, very close to the Po Valley, where the main cities of northern Italy are located. The capture of this zone would end the German occupation of the country and make it possible to reach the Alps and the border with Austria, very close to Germany. Despite it being clear that Allied victory was only a matter of time by the end of 1944, the Germans continued their resistance and a huge effort was necessary to force them to surrender.

Initial operations

On 31 October, when only 11 P-47Ds of the group were in service, the first Brazilian pilots began their operations, when the squadron commanders flew as wingmen on US squadrons to have their first war

Preparing the bombs. (Author's collection)

Torres' plane, the 42-26756, in a rare photograph taken air to air. After a collision with a C-47 during an air to air photo session, Moura forbade such pictures. (Author's collection)

The plane 42-26781 was destined for the FAB and received Brazilian colours on the wing but was finally sent to a USAAF unit. (Author's collection)

Lima Mendes, to the left with the mechanics of his plane, the 44-19660, baptized Rompe Mato by him. (Author's collection)

The oxygen mask was widely used because of the high cruise altitudes en route to the targets and the risk of contamination from carbon monoxide. (Author's collection)

Medeiros hears USAAF Captain Hugh 'Rowdy' Dow's description of a mission. (Author's collection)

experience. The first of them was Major Pamplona during a sortie by the 346th Squadron, taking off at 1305 and flying as wingman of the second element of the second escadrille, attacking a train station and damaging a locomotive. On the same day, Major Lafayette Cantarino Ribeiro de Souza and Captains Joel Miranda, Fortunato Câmara de Oliveira and Newton Lagares Silva also flew their first missions.

On 4 November, they flew again, Lieutenent-Colonel Nero Moura, commander of the group, and 1st Lieutenant Horácio Monteiro

Veteran pilots during the ferrying of the new Thunderbolts from the USA to Brazil after the war. (Author's collection)

Canário, Nero Moura and Lafayette at San Giusto airfield in March 1945. (Author's collection)

Yellow escadrille line up with rocket launchers and incendiary bombs built using 75-gallon fuel tanks. (Author's collection)

Machado performing their first missions.

On the following day, during the 17th mission which the unit undertook, for the first time two Brazilians took part, Nero Moura and Pamplona, both as wingmen of the second element of each escadrille of the 345th Fighter Squadron, which was performing its 668th mission, destroying a railway bridge.

Aspirant Fernando Corrêa Rocha remembered:

> My first mission [mission 22 for the unit] took place on 6 November 1944. I didn't expect to do a mission on that day, because they were performed by the captains. We prepared ourselves and went to the 347th Squadron. We were informed that it was a very dangerous mission. We were eight pilots, only two Brazilians and the others Americans. The photographs arrived and everyone examined them; I also took a look, but I could not see anything. It was an artillery position to the south of Bologna, in the mountains. This target was very close to the front-line, only one minute of flight. I flew as No-4 on one escadrille and 2nd Lieutenant John Richardson Cordeiro e Silva on the other [mission 21 of the unit]. We attacked the target and the other escadrille gained some distance to attack ahead of us. The target was the same zone. The flak opened fire over the first escadrille and when I dropped my bombs I don't know where they fell, as I didn't have the chance to look back. The recovery of our escadrille didn't let us gain altitude and immediately we began to strafe targets in Bologna at very low altitude. So, I followed them,

Mechanics of the 1st GAvCa in front of one of the Thunderbolts. (Author's collection)

USAF Major John Buyers with a mechanic during the preparation of a plane for a mission. (John Buyers)

From left to right: Torres, Goulart, Tormim Costa and Rui Moreira Lima. (John Buyers)

> firing at what they were firing at, without knowing too much what I was doing. That was when I heard the following conversation between two Americans: 'He's gone,' said one of them, and the other asked 'Who's gone?', and the other answered 'I think it was the Brazilian'. This fell like a bomb on me, as we were only two Brazilians on the escadrille. I immediately said 'No, I'm alive! So it was Cordeiro who died …' For me the mission was over. All that remained was only to return home and weep for the lost comrade. My first mission was terrible. This is one thing that hits me very deeply today.

Cordeiro was the first Brazilian pilot killed in combat, shot down by German flak while returning from the mission. The pilot informed his commander that he would try a forced landing close to Pianoro, but when his plane touched the ground it exploded.

The German flak was the only opposition to the planes, but it was terribly effective and well coordinated, so Allied losses were high and it was very usual to return with damage. Most of the guns were the 20mm *Rheinmetall- Borsig Flak L-38*, with a range of 4,900 metres.

On the following day, another loss occurred when 2nd Lieutenant Oldegard Olsen Sapucaia had an accident during a training flight in which simulated bombing and strafing missions were made over Via Aurelia. While recovering from a strafing run, Sapucaia made evasive manoeuvres with a very violent turn and the plane entered into a corkscrew with no control only 45 metres above the ground. The pilot jumped but could not open his parachute before hitting the ground. Because of this accident, the unit remained grounded until its cause could be determined.

Rui Moreira Lima, Torres and Goulart of the green, red and blue escadrilles respectively. (John Buyers)

Two days later, a notice from the constructor arrived, indicating that due to the shape of the bubble canopy of the P-47D, while doing violent manoeuvres with ailerons and rudder, the latter jammed, leading to an uncontrolled corkscrew. To fix this problem, a kit was provided to install a dorsal fin ahead of the tail, installed on the planes gradually by the 80th Service Squadron at Cercola, when they were sent for major repairs, while the planes received to replace losses arrived with the modification. However, some P-47Ds did not receive it.

Maintenance on a plane at Pisa. (Author's collection)

The plane serialled 4226758 was used by Assis in the Esquadrilha Verde. (Author's collection)

The plane of Rui Moreira Lima, 42-26786. (Author's collection)

Flying alone

Once the cause of Sapucaia's accident was found, and because the leaders of the escadrilles and the Group had some combat experience, independent operations of the *1º GAvCa* began from 11 November, with the radio call sign Jambock, while training flights continued. Initially they would only perform armed reconnaissance missions, armed only with machine guns.

The first flight (mission 26) took off at 0800, with eight P-47s divided into the *Vermelha* (Captain Laffayette, Lieutenants Keller, Kopp and Cox) and *Verde* escadrilles (Captain Pamplona, Lieutenants Coelho, Assis and Meira) to look for enemy planes around Bergamo, Verona and Mantova, but finding nothing.

The second flight of the day was formed by the *Azul* (Captain Câmara de Oliveira and 2nd Lieutenants Lima Mendes, Neiva de Figueiredo and Goulart Pereira) and *Amarelha* escadrilles (Captain Miranda, 1st Lieutenant Campos de Medeiros and 2nd Lieutenants Dornelles and Motta Paes), but they also did not find any target in the region they overflew, close to Lake Garda, and returned to base.

On the next day, during mission 28, they flew for the first time with three escadrilles, but the third had only three planes. Despite seeing some possible targets, they did not fire against them and on the return three planes had to land on the recently occupied aerodrome at Pisa due to lack of fuel. The next mission of the day was the first of the few with 12 Brazilian pilots, but again they found nothing to fire against.

On 13 November, there were two missions of 12 planes each, but

A German command post bombed by the Thunderbolts on 18 April. (Author's collection)

The railway bridge at Legnano destroyed by Thunderbolts. (Author's collection)

The pilots are taken to their planes before a mission. (Author's collection)

the second could not find anything because of bad weather, which impeded the flights on the next two days.

On the 16th another accident caused the loss of two Brazilian pilots. The Americans were making a propaganda documentary about the participation of the *1º GAvCa* and other Brazilian units in the war, to be shown in the Allied countries to promote their participation in the war. After making several takes on the ground they were to film some air-to-air shots from a USAAF C-47B, in which 2nd Lieutenants Roland Rittmeister and Waldyr Paulino Pequeño embarked to take some pictures of the P-47Ds in flight. The C-47 would fly at 5,000ft from north to south, with four P-47s making passes to the left of the plane. The Thunderbolts approached in a V formation, at double the speed of the C-47. When they were about to make the first pass, and

A mechanic examining a hole left by a bullet during a mission. (Author's collection)

German armoured vehicles and self-propelled artillery crossing the Po River in March 1945. (Author's collection)

The runway at Tarquínia in November 1944. (Author's collection)

The plane of Nero Moura, 42-26450. (Author's collection)

A train station under attack. (Author's collection)

A German command post attacked on 17 April. (Author's collection)

A railway destroyed by bombs. (Author's collection)

when the Thunderbolts were only 100 metres behind the C-47, the latter made a slight turn to the left. Captain Newton Lagares Silva, leader of the escadrille, tried to change course but he could not avoid the wingtip of the plane of 2nd Lieutenant Luis F. Perdigão Medeiros and hit the wing of the C-47. The pilot of the fighter managed to jump without problems, but the C-47 entered in a corkscrew and hit the ground, killing all the occupants.

The situation for the *1º GAvCa* was very bad, as in only 11 days they had lost four pilots, when the maximum acceptable was three in a month. In addition to this, only one of them was lost in combat, the other three in accidents.

On the next day, they flew again on two armed reconnaissance missions, followed by four on 18 November and five on the 19th, flying between four and 12 planes per mission.

Interdiction

On 21 November, the Group started interdiction missions armed with two 500lb (227kg) AN/M43 bombs over the Po Valley, 45 minutes of flight time from Tarquínia. These missions involved impeding the enemy's distribution of supplies to the front line and the movement of troops to the front from rearward positions. The missions consisted of dive bombings, with two flights of two planes each against the assigned target, diving from 9,000ft down to 4,500ft. After releasing their bombs, each flight returned alone at very low height, strafing targets when the opportunity arose using their eight Browning M2 12.7mm machine guns, which had a firing rate of 750-850 shots per minute, the planes having 267 shots for each gun. Such operations continued until the end of the war, and formed the majority of missions for the *1º GAvCa*.

An attack against a convoy of German vehicles in an Italian town. (Author's collection)

Fortunato after landing from a mission. (John Buyers)

An ammunition depot destroyed by the 1st GAvCa. (Author's collection)

The B-25C serial 41-12872, baptized Desert Lil and Earthquakers and used for transport missions. (Author's collection)

Major Nero Moura, in front of his plane. (Author's collection)

On some occasions, they also used AN/M65A1 250lb (118kg) general purpose bombs, 100lb (40kg) fragmentation ones or FTIs (Fuel Tank Incendiaries) of 340, 416 or 624 litres, which were adapted extra fuel tanks.

The first bombing mission was the second flight of the day (mission 46), with the escadrille *Amarela*, commanded by Nero Moura, and the *Vermelha*, headed by its commander, 1st Lieutenant Kopp. Most of the bombs did not hit the target, while one made a direct impact but probably did not explode, as no damage was seen. All of the planes of the *Amarela* except Moura (1st Lieutenants Campos de Medeiros and Ferreira da Costa and 2nd Lieutenant Lara de Araujo) were hit and had to land at Pisa, while Aspirant Pereyron of the *Vermelha* was hit and had to land at Siena.

First results

On 22 November, during mission 47, the *1º GAvCa* managed to hit their target for the first time, when they destroyed two railway bridges close to Legnano at 0940, each with two 500lb bombs. Two bombs also fell close to the target, but the other eight landed far from it. The next mission flew over its target at 1220 and made impacts with six to eight bombs on a fuel deposit at Modena, which was completely destroyed, the smoke reaching as high as 8,000ft. On the same day, six P-47s attacked a railway station at Cerea and destroyed part of it and two wagons, ending a successful day for the unit.

Two German ambulances can be seen bottom left on a road near Quistello. (Author's collection)

On 22 April the pilots located a camouflaged garage which they attacked many times destroying almost all the vehicles. (Author's collection)

Feeding the Browning M3 machine guns. (Author's collection)

Another view of the garage attacked on 22 April. (Author's collection)

Preparing the machine guns. (Author's collection)

On the following days, bad weather impeded more attacks, but on 25 November, on mission 52, they reached targets at Parma and to the west of Ferrara, while on the next day they performed attacks against train installations, but one had to be aborted over the target because the poor weather made it impossible to see the target. During this day, and the 29th and 30th of the same month, the railway running from Rimini to Parma was attacked, particularly between Parma and Bologna, while on mission 57 they attacked targets to the north, between Mantova and Verona, and on the 29th they could not find the target, again because of bad weather.

By the end of November, they had performed 59 combat missions without further losses, but by then the autumn rains had made the aerodrome virtually non-operational, so it was decided to transfer the 350th Fighter Group to San Giusto Airport in Pisa, which had been captured from the Germans. Despite the aerodrome being extensively bombed by the Allies, the runway was still operational, had better facilities and was only 50km from the front line. However, the hangars were destroyed and only small parts of them could be used. The move began on 2 December, without them discontinuing

Damage caused by flak to the plane serialled 42-26786. (Author's collection)

The Esquadrilha Verde in flight with another escadrille in the background. (Author's collection)

Close-up of damage caused by flak to the plane serialled 42-26786. (Author's collection)

Damage caused by a Thunderbolt attack recorded by the K-25 camera. (Author's collection)

Ground personnel prepare the weapons for a mission. (Author's collection)

their air operations, and finished two days later.

By then, 25 USAAF and RAF fighter squadrons were deployed in the north of Italy, including the Brazilians.

From 1 December, the attacks started to be carried out more to the north, bombing railways and bridges at Cremona (missions 61 and 62), Mantova (mission 60), Parma (mission 63) and Legnano (mission 65), but on mission 64 a non-identified target was attacked (probably a railway) close to Imola and one of the planes was hit by flak, causing minor damage.

10
PISA

Immediately after arrival at Pisa, the winter stopped the Allies' advance, and during early December the missions were reduced to finish the transfer to the new base. On 4 December, mission 68 took place, the first that landed back in Pisa: three missions were performed on 3 December, but the planes returned to Tarquínia.

On 5 December, only one mission was made (the 69th), the first made from Pisa, consisting of an attack on opportunity targets close to Bologna. On the following day, when returning from a mission close to Ghedi, to the south-west of Lake Garda, the planes of the escadrille *Azul*, commanded by Captain Câmara de Oliveira, landed back at Tarquínia because of bad weather, while of the four of *Vermelha*, commanded by Captain Lafayette Ribeiro de Souza, three landed at Malignano and one at Pontedera, very close to Pisa.

On 7 December, an attack took place around Parma, destroying a railway and returning to Pisa without problems. Flights were then suspended until the 10th, when three missions took place (72 to 74). During the first of these they attacked railways and at 1005 saw a jet airplane heading west at 16,000ft and at about 300-400mph, leaving a condensation contrail. Later they saw another plane heading north, at 15,000ft, over Bologna, which was identified as a probable P-38 Lightning. On the following mission of the day, another unidentified plane was spotted over Bologna, flying at about 25,000ft, leaving a condensation contrail. On the return they had to land at Pontedera because the runway at Pisa was already being used.

From the 13th, activity was increased again in missions 76 to 79, with two planes receiving damage on the first mission and one on the second, all caused by flak. On the last two missions the main target between Modena and Bologna could not be attacked, so they hit secondary targets close to La Spezia, only 50km from Pisa.

From then until 18 December, activity was very intense, with 25 missions in six days taking the total to 100 missions, some of them reaching the area of Trento in the Brenner Pass, on the border with Austria, the main point used by the Germans to send supplies to their troops fighting in Italy. One mission almost reached the border with Yugoslavia, but in the Brenner Pass many missions had to be suspended because it was common to find very bad weather there, impeding visibility and making it impossible to fly at low altitude between the mountains.

From 15 December, the *1º GAvCa* also performed escort missions to C-47s carrying supplies to special forces operating behind enemy lines, repeating such missions on the 17th (when they could not find the C-47s) and the 20th. In these cases they were only armed with machine guns and carried extra fuel tanks.

By this time, four planes had received K-25A oblique cameras on the leading edge of the left bomb pylon, replacing the original 16mm one installed on the right-wing root: the new one produced clearer results and made it possible to better see the results of the attacks. The first modified plane was the P-47D-25-RE serialled 42-26756, call sign A4, used by 2nd Lieutenant Alberto Martins Torres, with the work carried out by Brazilian mechanics. The cameras were used by the fourth plane of each escadrille on the attacks, which had to face the flak alone to take pictures of the targets.

Unlike US pilots, who returned home after 35 combat missions, the Brazilians could not change pilots. Only six pilots were sent to the unit as replacements during the whole war, the first of them arriving on 25 December 1944. While this led to the Brazilians having very great combat experience, because of the casualties suffered the quantity of disposable pilots was diminishing. Besides the pilots lost in combat and in accidents, seven had to be repatriated because of health problems. Because of this, Major Moura decided to train on the P-47 the three pilots who had not passed the exams in Panama and

An ammunition truck explodes during an attack by Thunderbolts. (Author's collection)

From left to right: Meira de Vasconcelos, Pessoa Ramos, Rocha, Coelho and Tormin. (Author's collection)

Damage caused to Perdigão's plane during his attack on 24 April when he passed through the ball of fire from the explosion of his target. (Author's collection)

Torres' plane at Tarquínia. (Author's collection)

were serving as radar controllers.

On 23 December, escadrilles *Amarela* and *Azul* performed an attack against train facilities in northern Italy (mission 106). On their return, the *Amarela* descended to search for opportunity targets, finding a train close to Isola di Scala. During the attack, 1st Lieutenant Ismael de Motta Paes was hit by flak and he had to parachute from his plane, and was taken prisoner and taken to *Stalag-Luft* 1 camp.

On 26 December, during mission 115, the P-47s used for the first time 110-gallon incendiary bombs, as well as 500lb bombs, during an air attack on the front line about 50km north of Pisa. Meanwhile,

The plane used by Canário when he hit a funnel during the mission. Despite the damage he managed to return. Here, Sergeants Araujo, de Almeida and Navarro show the remains of the wing of plane 44-19663/ A-6. (Author's collection)

The plane serialled 44-10854, damaged during a mission on 27 April, with Menezes at the controls. (Author's collection)

on 28 December, during mission 122, the first escort operations took place for 18 B-25J Mitchells in an attack on the north of the country, escorting them from Rimini to their target on the border with Austria. Close to Venice they saw a plane that attempted to attack the bombers, but immediately after, probably when the pilot saw the seven P-47s, he escaped in a dive.

On that day the first armed reconnaissance mission (number 123) also took place, flying Lieutenant Colonel Wanderley and Captain Pamplona Pinto close to the front line, to the north of Pisa. It was repeated on the following day, as well as an escort mission for 20 B-25s which bombed targets in the Brenner Pass.

By the end of December, the Brazilians had performed 134 combat missions, with a minimum pilot availability of 77 per cent and an average of 81 per cent. As a Christmas present, the unit received the B-25C Mitchell serial 41-12872 and baptised 'Desert Lil' and 'Earthquakers', for use in transport flights.

1945

On 2 January 1945, the *Esquadrilha Amarela* took off on another armed reconnaissance and bombing mission in the Piacenza, Brescia, Turin and Genoa area (mission 138). They attacked a railway bridge on the Vara River and later returned, searching for opportunity targets. At Alessandria, they attacked a train at the station, despite heavy flak fire. The last plane of the escadrille, piloted by 1st Lieutenant João Maurício Campos de Medeiros, was hit and the pilot announced he would jump. His comrades watch him jump and deduced he was made prisoner, but when the war ended they learned that he died when falling over high tension lines.

They had started to fly missions more to the west of the valley of the Po River, closer to Milan and Genoa.

On 3 January, they performed another escort mission to 36 B-25s over the Brenner Pass, but also attacked railway facilities close to Rovereto. Another long-range mission took place on 15 January, when they reached Pordenone, Treviso, Mestre and Venice, in the north-east of the country, during missions 164 and 165, something repeated in the next two missions two days later. After that, on 20 and 21 January they attacked the area surrounding Milan.

On the 22nd, while they continued attacking that zone, another pilot was shot down: 1st Lieutenant Aurélio Vieira Sampaio was hit by flak and later died. On 25 January, during mission 181, the planes attacked train facilities close to Turin, reaching the most westerly point of their missions until then.

The loss of Sampaio was followed on 29 January by 1st Lieutenant Josino Maia de Assis (on mission 188), who after attacking a fuel depot close to Piacenza, was hit by 37mm fire and had to parachute from his plane. After being rescued by partisans, he was captured by the Germans. Better luck was enjoyed by Aspirante Raymundo da Costa Canário who, on 27 January, during an attack by the *Esquadrilha Amarela*, hit a chimney and lost 1.28 metres of his plane's right wing, but despite this severe damage he made it back to Pisa. Canário, at 18 years old, was the youngest pilot of the unit.

A few days later, on 31 January, during mission 194 targeting the aerodrome at Ghedi, they damaged a single *Aer*Macchi *202* and one *Messerschmitt Me-210*, while they saw about 15 other planes - Junkers *Ju-87*s, *Messerschmitt Bf-109*s and *Me-210*s - in one of the few missions they made against aircraft on the ground. On the same day, mission 196 was made, escorting two formations of B-25s, one of 18 planes and the other of 39, who bombed targets in the Brenner Pass. The P-47s also bombed targets around Trento.

Because of bad weather, the quantity of missions in January was smaller, with 61 flown. This situation continued in February, but the number of missions increased progressively, reaching a total of 346 for the whole war by the end of that month. Meanwhile, a spring offensive was being prepared, in an attempt to break the German front in the Po Valley and force their retreat to Austria. By this time, the fall of Germany was close and they started to negotiate with the Allies for a ceasefire, but without positive results.

Planes being prepared for a mission at Tarquínia. (Author's collection)

The plane of Fortunato, 42-26762, ready for a mission with bombs and rockets. (Author's collection)

Damage to the plane of Moreira Lima, 42-26786, on his mission of 29 April over the Brenner Pass. (Author's collection)

Damage to Perdigão's plane from his attack on 24 April when he passed through the ball of fire from his exploding target. (Author's collection)

The B-25C Desert Lil. (John Buyers)

John Buyers on the wing of Corrêa Netto's plane. (John Buyers)

The Esquadrilha Azul preparing for a mission. (John Buyers)

February

During the first days of February, normal operations continued, with more emphasis on the area around Lake Garda, near the border with Yugoslavia, as well as the Brenner Pass.

Testing of a new weapon to be used on the Brazilian Thunderbolts, the M10 disposable rocket launcher, began this month. This consisted of three tubes for 4.1in (105mm) M8A2 rockets, with the intention of increasing considerably the firepower of the planes. On 18 January, one P-47D-30-RE and the P-47D-25-RE serial 42-26450, call sign 1, of Major Moura, were sent for modifications to the AAFSC/MTO at Naples, where the works lasted between three and 10 days, installing the launching system below the wings, the electrical system and the control on the cockpit. By 3 April, the P-47D-27-RE serial 42-26786, call sign D4, had its modification completed, making a total of 28 planes with this capacity. Despite the high destructive power of the rockets against vehicles, their lack of precision made them unpopular among the pilots: the fins that maintained the direction of the rocket did not always open all at the same time.

On 22 February, during mission 231, the escadrilles *Amarelha* and *Verde* saw a plane close to Brescia, identified as a possible *Bf-109*, which escaped with evasive manoeuvres. That day, the other two escadrilles escorted a formation of B-25s to the Brenner Pass, which was repeated two days later and on the 27th. Meanwhile, on the 25th, the planes performed an armed reconnaissance (mission 240) which took them to Bolzano, almost at the border with Austria.

During February, five planes were shot down, but all pilots survived. On the 4th of the month, Captain Joel Miranda departed as commander of *Esquadrilha Amarela* to attack a railway. Near Castelfranco, he and 2nd Lieutenant Danilo Marques Moura (brother of the Group's commander) were shot down and had to jump. Miranda was found by Italian partisans, who protected him until the end of the war. Meanwhile, Moura spent 28 days on the run from the enemy until, after travelling for 340km, he made it across the lines and returned to his comrades.

On 10 February, during another flight of the *Esquadrilha Amarela*, 1st Lieutenant Roberto Brandini was shot down close to Rovigo. The pilot managed to jump and injured his head when he hit the ground, and was sent to a hospital by the Germans. On 15 February, Aspirante Canário was shot down and parachuted from his plane, being rescued by Brazilian troops of the FEB.

On the 20th, the *1º GAvCa* had the opportunity to directly support the FEB, which had been trying to take Monte Casteo since 24 November 1944. The planes bombed enemy troops which were threatening the flank of the troops in Mazzancana. Monte Castelo was finally captured on the next day.

By the end of the month, Major Nero Moura had to disband the *Esquadrilha Amarela* because of the lack of pilots, distributing the remaining ones to the other escadrilles. This escadrille had suffered the most casualties. By the end of the month, the Brazilian unit had only 28 pilots, while the average of the other squadrons of the group was 45.

On 3 March, on mission 250 of the *Esquadrilha Azul*, they escorted three C-47s that were to perform a paratroop drop close to Piacenza, but although the planes reached the target the Thunderbolts saw no jumps from the C-47s.

On the previous day, they discovered a number of ammunition depots at Suzzara, and it was decided to attack them. However,

Miranda Corrêa baptized his plane with the name of his wife and painted a pin-up girl on the fuselage but Nero Moura asked him to delete them. (Author's collection)

Intelligence officer Miranda Corrêa indicates a target during a briefing. (Author's collection)

Major Nero Moura descending from his plane. (Author's collection)

the German flak was still very effective and on 7 March, during mission 260, it shot down Captain Teobaldo Antonio Kopp, leader of *Esquadrilha Vermelha*, while attacking those depots after escorting the B-25s to Rovoreto. Parachuting safely, Kopp was found by Italian partisans who hid him until 21 April, when due to the Allied advance he was able to cross the front line and rejoin his comrades.

2º Ten.-Av. da res. conv. Armando de Souza Coelho. (Author's collection)

On the 8th, another escort mission was made for B-25s attacking Trento, and on their return they bombed railways and wagons, while on the 13th, 18th and 19th the escort mission was repeated.

On 11 March, 1st Lieutenant Rui Moreira Lima took off as part of *Esquadrilha Verde*, under the command of Captain Newton Lagares Silva, to attack the railway bridge at Casarsa, over the Madduna River, which was heavily defended by German flak. When he started his bombing run, Moreira Lima discovered an 88mm *Krupp* gun about 200 metres from the bridge and went in to attack it. When he was at 3,000ft, his engine was hit, losing two cylinders catching fire. The pilot still managed to hit the gun with his machine guns and later dropped his bombs on the bridge, hitting a train full of ammunition that was crossing it. The explosion further damaged the Thunderbolt, and Moreira Lima realised it was impossible to return to base, so he informed Lagares Silva of the situation:

> 'Jambock *Verde*, Jambock *Verde* 3, I will jump. I have no visibility because as well as the fire, there is oil on the windscreen, covering the canopy and I have smoke on the cockpit.'
>
> 'You are not going to jump, the flak will hit you on your descent. Put heading 150º and I will let you know when to jump,' was the reply.
>
> 'And the fire?'

Bombs and rockets being prepared for a mission. (Author's collection)

A US film team records the preparation of a Brazilian Thunderbolt for a propaganda documentary. (Author's collection)

Preparing a bomb fuse. (Author's collection)

Mechanics carrying out maintenance to the plane, serialled 42-26766, used by Dornelles. (Author's collection)

'It's an order, don't jump, there is a lot of flak surrounding your plane, they are hunting you.'

'Ok, Jambock *Verde*, take me to another plane, the canopy is starting to melt and I think I'm going to die!'

'Now, jump, you are over the Adriatic Ocean. I already asked for rescue. In two hours you will have a Catalina that will rescue you. Use your head and the life raft well!'.

Moreira Lima then tried to manoeuvre the plane to extinguish the flames, reducing power and diving until the fire was extinguished, and then restarting the engine, informing Lagares Silva of his decision. He recalled:

> My decision fell like a bomb among the escadrille. Among the words I heard they called me 'jackass', they said I would be burned, that I was afraid to jump. I heard them but I didn't pay attention.

However, the manoeuvre was successful and the pilot was guided to the aerodrome of the city of Forli, recently captured and used by the RAF.

He made a belly landing and Moreira Lima abandoned the plane with only an injured eye, burned by the hot oil while trying to look outside with the canopy opened and without his goggles. For this mission, he was awarded the Distinguished Flying Cross and was flying again two days later.

On 20 March, during mission 285, the Brazilians went further to the north in the Brenner Pass, attacking targets around Bressanone. Three days later, when the escadrilles *Azul* and *Vermelha* performed mission 291 to destroy the rail bridge of Montebelluna, one of them used the 4.1in rockets for the first time, as well as the 500lb bombs, with six rockets on each plane and making five impacts on two different targets. On the next day, they made two escort missions during an attack by the B-25s on the Brenner Pass.

By this time, the targets were in both the Po Valley and the Brenner Pass, successfully continuing their mission to weaken the German defences. Another loss took place on 26 March, when 1st Lieutenant Othon Corrêa Neto was hit by 20mm guns during a mission with the Esquadrilha *Azul* at Casarsa. He jumped from his plane and was captured. This mission, the 297th, was the second with rockets, firing 18 of the 24 carried by each escadrille, but they could not see if they hit the targets.

Later, on 29 March, during mission 299, they destroyed a ship on a river, in one of the few missions of this kind. On the following day, during mission 300, they used rockets again, firing 24 over a sugar refinery at Sermide, but 20 failed to hit the target. On that day, they

A Thunderbolt fires against some vehicles on a road. (Author's collection)

Rui Moreira Lima and Tormim Costa at Pisa. (John Buyers)

Torres' plane during a mission over northern Italy. (Author's collection)

escorted 36 B-25 Mitchells with eight P-47s, and on their return two planes escorted a damaged Mitchell which was hit by flak, until over Lake Veneta the six crew members jumped from the plane. On 31 March, eight planes performed another mission with rockets, firing 20 of the 48 they were carrying, and on the other mission of the day they escorted 54 B-25s to the Brenner Pass.

By the last days of the month, in which they reached 304 combat missions and with the spring offensive getting closer, they started to perform armed reconnaissance missions, attacking several kinds of targets, especially vehicles, railroads, roads and bridges.

The missions of the group were being increased, despite the lack of pilots. On 2 April, on mission 308, they used rockets again against two ammunition and one fuel storage, but could not see any impact. They made another escort mission for 36 B-25s on 5 April.

The use of rockets continued giving bad results, and on the 6th another mission was made with them by 2nd Lieutenant Meira de Vasconcelos and Aspirante Tormin Costa, hitting the target with their bombs but failing to see any impact of the rockets launched against explosive stores close to Fidenza. However, on the next mission (the 319th), 2nd Lieutenants Lara de Araujo and Coelho Magalhães managed to hit the target with most of the 11 rockets fired.

On 7 April, eight planes took off for mission 320 against a fuel refinery at Montechino, but when they arrived over the target they saw it was already being attacked by USAAF P-47Ds and P-40s, so they searched for another target. Near Piacenza, they attacked ammunition dumps, destroying 25 of them, the explosion from the last one damaging the plane of the leader, 1st Lieutenant Luiz Lopes Dornelles. On their return, they also destroyed a vehicle and damaged three train wagons.

11

THE SPRING OFFENSIVE

On 9 April, when the spring had just started, the long-awaited offensive began, with the forces of the Fifth US Army progressing to the Po Valley from the west while the Eighth British Army did so from the east, heading for the Yugoslav and Austrian border. During this period, the commander of the 350th Fighter Group transferred to the Brazilians the resposibility to select ground targets in a zone 30km wide and a depth equal to the range of the Thunderbolt, which reached the Austrian border. During that phase, the P-47s halted their attacks against railways, roadways and stores, which were their main tasks until then, to concentrate on attacking the front line and the forces giving support to fighting units, bombing trenches, artillery positions, command posts and vehicles moving through the zone,

The plane, serialled 42-26788, used by Kopp. (Author's collection)

Captain Fortunato in March 1945. (John Buyers)

Goulart on the wing of his plane in March 1945. (John Buyers)

A dive attack against a fuel depot near Avigliano on 31 March. (Author's collection)

among other targets.

Second Lieutenant Alberto Martins Torres remembered:

> A few days after the spring offensive was launched, the intelligence and operations officers began to exclaim 'The Hun is on the run'. The Germans had begun a monumental retreat all across the Po Valley. On each route heading north, hundreds of vehicles, waggons, tanks and walking troops fled from the Allied tanks which were descending from the Apennines, spearheading the big offensive.

According to Lieutenant José Rebelo Meira de Vasconcelos:

> The retreat was reasonably organized. It was a fast retreat looking for the Alpine passes going from Italy to Austria. The Germans retreated with complete units, in formation and defended [themselves]. Their main worry was to be out of Italy as fast as possible. This obligated them to pass through some confluence areas, like road crossings, bridges and mountain passes, and that's where we would fall on them.

The intensification of attacks also led to an increase in losses. On 9 April, 2nd Lieutenant Armando de Souza Coelho was shot down and fell close to Pádua. He managed to parachute from his plane shortly after crossing the front line, and was rescued by Allied forces and returned to his base.

Four days later, the *Esquadrilha Azul* attacked a bridge close to Casarsa and on their return started to strafe an ammunition depot close to Spilimbergo. During one of the strafing passes, when Aspirante Frederico Gustavo dos Santos was firing at one of the depots, one of them exploded with such force that it destroyed his plane, which turned upside down. The pilot tried to escape, but it was impossible and he died with his plane.

On 14 April, during mission 333, the Brazilians launched 24 rockets against a pontoon bridge on the Po River and damaged at least three pontoons, while on the following mission they launched 23 rockets against two ammunition depots, a railway station and an artillery position between Modena and Bologna, achieving impacts on all but the last target. On mission 335 they launched 21 rockets against the Gestapo headquarters in Bologna, with 15 hits, but they did not see any damage; however, they later hit the building with two bombs and machine-gun fire. They could not see any result of their rocket attacks during the following mission, when they attacked an Italian command post to the south of Vignola, despite 14 rockets striking the target.

From this time, rockets were used on all sorties, with results improving appreciably, especially in attacks against troop concentrations or large-scale targets, where precision was not too important.

On the same day, the *Esquadrilha Azul* performed the first sortie (mission 337) with T.8 90lb fragmentation cluster bombs, each plane also carrying six rockets, successfully attacking an artillery position close to Vignola. Later, on the last mission of the day, they used 500lb bombs and rockets again, attacking an ammunition depot between Modena and Bologna.

The number of missions increased despite the lack of pilots in the *1º GAvCa*, with an average of four to six until 21 April, concentrating their efforts on the area around Vignola, to the south of Modena and

Reloading the 12.7mm machine guns. (John Buyers)

Torres' plane after the mission of 29 April during which it was severely damaged. (Author's collection)

German transport vehicles destroyed by Thunderbolts; seen from a plane with a K-25 camera on a very low pass. (Author's collection)

The scene at Pisa: full of USAAF and Brazilian planes. (Author's collection)

Bologna, on the front line. Using 500lb bombs and rockets, as well as 110-gallon napalm canisters on mission 342 on 15 April, missions 345 and 346 on the 16th and the 350th on the following day, they had a devastating effect, especially in the last attack against German trenches, which were strafed after using the napalm and rockets.

On 18 April, during mission 354 by *Esquadrilha Azul*, they used napalm again, as it had proved very effective against infantry positions and constructions where Germans resisted the Allied advance.

On 19 April, the German front was broken and Allied forces started their advance through the Po Valley. Because of this, the *1º GAvCa* performed two armed reconnaissance missions more to the north-west that day, between Brescia and Palma and to Lake Garda, while on the 20th they made three missions of this kind between Modena and Bologna.

One day later, while taking off for a mission, Captain Roberto Pessoa Ramos went off the runway because of technical failures and the landing gear collapsed, writing off the plane, but the pilot escaped unhurt. During the first mission of the day (number 368), in which for the first time they used only rockets and machine guns, without bombs, the *Esquadrilha Vermelha* saw many troops retreating to the north, leaving Modena. They attacked them, especially two guns towed by horses and two tanks, one of which was damaged by machine-gun fire after the rockets failed to hit it while the other was destroyed, together with many other vehicles, including ambulances. The pilots also saw many Allied tanks advancing to the north behind the Germans.

During the next mission, commanded by Lieutenant Colonel Nero Moura, with Aspirante Costa Canário as wingman, they attacked some military vehicles at Carpi, to the north of Modena, confirming what the other escadrille saw. They were followed by the flight of 2nd Lieutenants Neiva de Figueireido and Goulart Pereira, who attacked two vehicles, launching three rockets without success, but then destroyed them with machine guns. They also flew without bombs on these two missions. On the next one, 2nd Lieutenants Torres and Keller flew armed with rockets and napalm canisters, destroying several vehicles. At 1950 that day, the planes saw that the Allied spearhead had just reached Route 9, which runs from Bologna to Modena, and was progressing fast to the north.

One day later, the dramatic situation on the front line led to a major participation by Brazilian planes, in what was later remembered as 'Fighter Aviation Day'.

22 April, 1945

The pace of the German retreat was increasing, using all kind of vehicles to head north, including horse-towed waggons, cars, trucks and requisitioned civilian buses. The Allies needed to secure a bridgehead on the north side of the Po before the Germans could consolidate their positions there. The best way to impede the Germans in northern Italy was to destroy their equipment at the points where they crossed the rivers, which was where they would be most vulnerable. The Allied command therefore asked all aviation units for maximum effort

A bridge being attacked by Thunderbolts during the Italian winter. (Author's collection)

Nero Moura's plane, serialled 42-26450. (Author's collection)

Soldier Eurides Cardoso Pereira finishes his work to prepare the fuse of a bomb before a mission while 2º Sergeant Fernando Gonçalves de Azevedo checks the landing hear. (Author's collection)

between 21-24 April. Despite the Brazilians only having 22 pilots and 23 planes, they did all they could to accomplish their mission, flying between two and three sorties per pilot on 22 April.

The first sortie, planned for sunrise, was cancelled due to lack of visibility, but at 0830 the Thunderbolts of the three escadrilles began to take off, each armed with two 500lb bombs. This was to be an armed reconnaissance mission in the area of routes 40 and 70, looking for enemy vehicles. At 0910 the attacks began, the first of them by *Esquadrilha Azul* against a pontoon bridge, But due to heavy 20mm and 88mm flak they could not aim and missed the target. After that they saw about 20 similar bridges, and on their return saw many soldiers on foot and in vehicles, but they continued looking for better targets. Captain Horácio Machado Monteiro saw a large group of tanks and, as they did not have the yellow markings used by Allied tanks for identification, he assumed they were German. The forward controller of the 350th Fighter Group ordered him to attack, because there was no information about Allied tanks in that area, but a pass at lower altitude allowed them to be identified as US Army M-4 Sherman tanks. Despite the insistence of the command to attack the tanks, Monteiro refused to do so and later saw that some of them were carrying the yellow markings, so ordered the return to base. It was later discovered that they were a group of US Sherman tanks which had broken through the front line and were advancing at high speed inside enemy territory, taking advantage of the German retreat.

Second Lieutenant Armando de Souza Coelho, in his plane with Cabo Alvaro de Oliveira Gigante. (Author's collection)

Meanwhile, the other two escadrilles performed the first attacks of the day close to Suzarra, in the case of *Esquadrilha Verde* destroying several houses and later some vehicles while returning. The *Vermelha* attacked a bridge and then continued to their secondary target, Suzarra train station, where they destroyed some track and wagons.

At 0945 the fourth sortie took off, under the command of Lieutenant Colonel Nero Moura, including USAAF Captain John Buyers (who flew 22 missions with the Brazilians), armed only with machine guns, as they were during the rest of the day. Close to San Benedetto they found a concentration of about 80-100 vehicles, which they attacked, destroying several and leaving a smoke column that reached 500 metres. Second Lieutenant Renato Goulart Pereira recalled:

> We found that target by accident. We were at the height we used to search, ready to attack anything that appeared in front of us when Neiva gave the alert. We started doing passes, strafing what we could see in front of us. We entered at very low altitude and when the target was 350 or 400 metres in front of us we opened fire with our machine guns, which were prepared so the bullets converged at that distance.

Buyers also remembered:

> I was number 2 and I dived behind Nero. The park, full of vehicles, was too attractive a target to worry about the flak. Our planes were separated, one on each side of the rectangle, as if we were

The new Thunderbolts arrived at Campo dos Afonsos after being ferried from the USA.

Nero Moura briefing pilots before a mission. The Brazilian pilots used a light flight jacket and carried a .45 pistol on their missions.

M-8 rockets flying to their target. (Author's collection)

> on a shooting range, turning around the target. Suddenly I heard something like a ra-ta-ta, as if a machine gun was firing beside my plane, but I saw nothing because I was concentrated on the targets I was attacking. That was when I heard the voice of Neiva: 'Buyers! They are firing at you!' Then I sarted to see the tracers converging around my plane. The alarm was so great that I vomited inside my mask. I had to continue the mission at the same time I was cleaning my face.

While this escadrille was landing, at 1055 the *Verde* took off again, commanded by 1st Lieutenant Rui Moreira Lima, who attacked again the vehicles strafed by the former escadrille and enemy trenches to the west of Nogara. They also saw many barges crossing the Po and other rivers to the west of Borgoforte, but did not attack them as they had no more ammunition. One thing they noticed was the large quantity of ambulances heading north, which led them to suppose they were actually carrying troops in a bid to save them from attacks by the Thunderbolts.

At 1140 the *Azul* escadrille took off and also headed to San Benedetto, where they destroyed at least 15 trucks and a house, while they also destroyed another two houses on their return. Continuing their raid at low altitude, they found a convoy of horse-towed wagons, which was strafed, destroying at least 30 of them and causing heavy casualties. When the escadrille was returning, at 1240 the *Vermelha* took off again; apart from 2nd Lieutenant Torres, the pilots were performing their second mission of the day. By then, the German retreat was widespread and disordered, so the mission had no more assigned targets: they were only ordered to go to the Po Valley and attack whatever they found.

During this mission, the weather was worsening, but visibility was still good. During the flight, they found many camouflaged vehicles close to buildings occupied by the Germans, which were destroyed. They also damaged two rafts and other vehicles. Like the other escadrilles, they also saw a lot of ambulances.

They were followed at 1345 by the *Verde* again, which attacked the same vehicle concentration, but without seeing any evidence they had destroyed anything. At 1445, the ninth mission of the day followed, again under the command of Nero Moura, strafing 16 vehicles and destroying 13 of them. The 10th mission of the day took off at 1515, the *Verde* escadrille returning after destroying a light tank, a command vehicle and a building. By then, the weather was much worse, with very low clouds.

Until then they had performed 40 take-offs in 10 missions (372 to 381) without any losses, but on the last mission of the day (the 382nd), made by the *Esquadrilha Azul*, which took off at 1545, 2nd Lieutenant Marcos Eduardo Coelho de Magalhães was shot down while attacking two tanks and some trucks: he jumped from his plane and was captured. One of the other planes was severely damaged but managed to return to base. However, during this mission they destroyed 21 vehicles carrying ammunition and damaged another five. At 2045 the remaining planes landed, ending operations for the day. During 22 April, they had destroyed or severely damaged a total of 97 motor

Ground crews preparing the bombs for a mission. (Author's collection)

Green Escadrille planes. Lagares' first plane. (Author's collection)

The 4125 (serialled 44-21093) in Brazil, after the war. (Author's collection)

transport, 35 animal-towed vehicles and 14 buildings occupied by the enemy, damaging another 17 motor vehicles and two bridges and attacking another four enemy positions.

The last days

Despite the high rate of missions the previous day, there was no rest on 23 April, with another 10 missions and 39 take-offs. At 0600, the first planes took off, the *Esquadrilha Verde* destroying many vehicles. Forty-five minutes later, the *Vermelha* took off, with the same results, followed at 0750 by the *Azul*, also destroying several vehicles and watching Allied troops close to Ferrara and Scandiano, only a few kilometres from Modena. At 0855, the *Verde* took off again, flying close to the Po River.

On the next sortie, mission 387, the *Esquadrilha Vermelha* took off at 0930, using 500lb bombs again, three planes attacking vehicles and tanks to the north of Suzarra, while they saw a lot of German troops around the city heading north, looking for the Po River. At 1150, the second mission for the *Azul* began, with three planes destroying vehicles near Parma. The *Verde* took off again at 1255 on its third mission of the day, in which all the pilots flew for the second time that day (Captain Pessoa Ramos, 1st Lieutenant Moreira Lima and 2nd Lieutenant Correa Rocha had flown on the first mission, and 2nd Lieutenant Tormin Costa on the second). They attacked vehicles along the Po between Sermide and Ostiglia, which was where the *Vermelha* headed when they took off at 1445, destroying numerous horse-drawn wagons and causing many casualties, seeing that the Germans were retreating in a highly disorganized manner.

On mission 391, four planes, guided by Nero Moura, flew with 500lb bombs again on an armed reconnaissance to the north of the Po, while on the last sortie of the day the *Esquadrilha Vermelha* flew armed with rockets on an attack against a fuel depot close to Mantova.

On that day two planes were damaged by flak, those of 1st Lieutenant Rui Moreira Lima and 2nd Lieutenant Paulo Costa. The latter was flying the P-47D serial 42-26772, which, despite having the B1 call sign, the badge of the unit and Brazilian camouflage, still had the USAAF badge on its wings, which were not yet modified with the FAB colours. This plane was with the *1º GAvCa* for some time, replacing the previous B1, serialled 42-26759, which was lost on 4 February.

On 24 April, the attacks continued from 0645, with armed reconnaissance sorties all over the Po Valley. On the third mission, the planes of *Esquadrilha Verde* made an attack against a railway between Verona and Peschiera, finding about 100 wagons. Second Lieutenant Vasconcelos remembered that the leader of the escadrille, 1st Lieutenant Perdigão, said, 'How many wagons! I will descend to attack.' Vasconcelos continued:

> I answered, 'Perdigão, the Germans never left a single wagon in a railway yard … how could they have left more than 20?' He replied that this wasn't important and that he would take a look. I stayed flying around and watching his attack. He was lucky, because he opened fire at some distance. I saw the dust of the bullets reaching the target when suddenly the whole floor trembled and all the wagons exploded at the same time, something very violent. All who were flying over the Po Valley said the smoke reached 9,000ft. It was so violent that Perdigão, with no possibility of escaping, passed through the fire of the explosion. On the other side, he exclaimed, 'I'm almost blind, I can't see anything.' We answered him and he started to recover. On the wingtips, the plastic cover for the lights was completely melted and a part of the plane remained completely black. He was saved because the explosion was so big that the debris

Lieutenant Colonel Nelson Freire Lavénère Wanderley was the liaison offcer with the 12th Air Force but flew 13 missions with the unit. (John Buyers)

Mechanics cleaning the machine guns of a Thunderbolt. (Author's collection)

The plane, serialled 44-19661, piloted by Assis on a mission during 21 January. On this mission he was heavily damaged by flak close to Cassano and had to jump. He was rescued by partisans but was later made a prisoner by the Germans. (Author's collection)

passed before he entered the smoke and fire. On the film of his camera we saw a lot of debris passing in front of the plane.

First Lieutenant Perdigão returned safely to base, but the Thunderbolt was severely damaged.

On the following mission, the planes flew again with bombs, attacking artillery positions and railways, while they watched a jet airplane flying very high and heading north. Later, between Parma and Casalmagiore, 6.5km to the south of the Po, they saw Allied troops. In that area the Allies were advancing on a big scale, and in the following missions everyone reported watching US troops progressing close to Parma, while Suzarra and other towns close to it were occupied by the Allies, who had reached the south bank of the Po. By the end of the day, while the missions continued (10 for the whole day) they started to find less German activity.

The next day, they again flew 10 missions (numbers 403 to 412), starting at 0620 with an armed reconnaissance by the *Esquadrilha Azul*, from Milan to the Brenner Pass, finding only a few targets. They were followed by the *Verde*, which bombed railways close to Verona, while the *Vermelha* destroyed vehicles close to Vilafranca and saw that German troops were still to the south of the Po at Casalmagiore. On the next mission it was verified that the Germans were preparing their resistance in the foothills of the Alps, with trenches facing south in all the cities between Verona and Brescia.

During mission 407, commanded by Nero Moura, they performed another armed reconnaissance in western Italy, flying over Turin and then continuing to Milan, seeing almost no enemy activites in that zone, mainly because the Germans were retreating to the Alps to cross into Austria.

On the first mission of 26 April, the last pilot of the unit was lost,

The 4125 (44-21093) in Brazil after the war. (Author's collection)

Badge and missions on a P-47. (Author's collection)

The Green Flight at Pisa. (Author's collection)

The last plane with a B6 code; 42-28986 of Yellow flight. (Author's collection)

The plane of the operations chief of the 1st GAvCa, 44-21093, first used by Pamplona and later by Lagares. (Author's collection)

Tormin flying the plane, 44-21093 of Lagares. (Author's collection)

the leader of *Esquadrilha Vermelha*, 1st Lieutenant Dornelles; 2nd Lieutenant Torres remembered:

> We took off without a determined target. Dornelles flew over La Spezia and followed the railway that ended in Milan. It was an important communications and supply line and those were the places we were looking for. We reached Alessanria at the same time a train was reaching the station. I was No.3 on the escadrille and Dornelles left the formation, flying low because there was flak. He went to attack the train, No.2 behind him; I went also and my wingman behind me. However, when Dornelles passed, he was hit and exited in flames, falling close to the city. I shouted to No.2, 'Get in from another angle!', so he could avoid being hit. It was a sad end for Dornelles. His loss was very sad for all of us, as we knew the end of the war was very close.

On that day, air activity was reduced to only six missions, because the Germans were reaching the Brenner Pass and offered only minor resistance to the advance of the Allies, who had crossed the Po River and were entering the city of Verona, just to the south of the Alps. Most of the missions were concentrated to the north of Verona, close to Bussolengo, only a few kilometres to the east of Lake Garda, where the Germans were concentrating on their retreat to Austria.

The German defeat was close, and the commander of their forces in Italy and southern Germany, Marshal Albert Kesselring, said that after the Po crossing, their troops were not an army anymore. On 27 April, the cities of Alessandria, Milan, Geneva and Turin were occupied,

The plane of Nero Moura along with the Red Flight. (Author's collection)

but there was still much resistance and the Brazilians continued performing many sorties, now adding many of close air support at the request of the ground forces, known as Rover Pete after the call sign of the ground controller. They also still had to face very intense flak.

On that day, they flew only four missions, all around Padova, on one of them using 500lb bombs, while on the others they used only machine guns, as in most missions at that time.

On the following day, during their first sortie (mission 423), they watched Allied tanks approaching Vincenza, while on mission 425 over the west of Italy they saw there was no more German presence, only civilians waving Italian or white flags. On the fourth and final mission, as the ground controller (Rover Pete) had no targets, they attacked vehicles at Bassano, to the north of Vincenza, and on their return they had to land at Forli due to lack of fuel.

On 29 April, they performed eight missions, on what was the last day of major activity. On the second sortie, they attacked a small enemy column at Bassano, where Allied forces were approaching at the start of the Alps. Those were the last German forces found in that area. On their return, they flew over the aerodrome of Ghedi, which was recently occupied by the Allies.

On the fourth mission (number 430), 1st Lieutenant Moreira Lima was flying as No.3 on an escadrille with Nero Moura, Buyers and Rocha to bring close air support. Lima remembered:

> After dropping the bombs we went to perform a close air support mission. We went to the Brenner Pass, where there was a road that connected the pass with Lake Garda and a few kilometres ahead were three Tiger tanks in camouflaged positions that had stopped the Allied advance. When we arrived over the place we made contact with Rover Jo (the forward controller) and we gave them our possition. When we were circling above, I saw the camouflage and alerted Nero Moura, who told me he also saw the tanks. Nero asked me to wait and immediately he said, 'Now you're going to attack and you have the command of the escadrille.' When I went in I did it a little bit wrong, confused by the heat of combat, and I must have passed Lake Garda from east to west. But I wanted to attack and I went in in a way that if I was hit I didn't have any way to exit, and that was what happened. There was heavy fire; it was about 1600 and the sun was already behind the mountains and the valley was very dark. After I went in I said on the radio, 'Don't go in because there is heavy fire and the space is very small!' Then I made the attack on the first tank: the tactic is to attack from below and behind, that way the incendiary ammunition hits the tank and burns it. I told Rover Jo that we only had machine guns and to attack a tank with them is very complicated. Then I received a message from him saying 'it's worth exchanging the plane for the tank'. So I burned that tank, but I received a hit, I don't know which calibre, exactly on the six oxygen bottles of my plane. The hit was strong. I don't know if the shot came from the tank, but the explosion of the bullet and the oxygen made me think the plane was in flames, but it was only a scare. I was at a very high speed and

Photo taken on 13 March during a mission over the Brenner Pass headed by Lagares. (Author's collection)

> I went to the second tank, which was difficult to fire at, but I hit it. With the two targets destroyed I went for the third one, leaving all three out of service. But when I finished my attack my speed wasn't so fast, so I pulled my stick to climb and return. The place where I was was very narrow. I had to make a very tight turn and when I reached a speed that was safe for the plane (140 or 150mph) the wing fell as if I had lost control. I immediately exclaimed, 'I lost the controls!' I released the canopy and when it fell Rocha told Nero, 'Rui jumped but the parachute didn't open!' But I hadn't jumped yet; I still had the headphones on. I threw them on the floor of my plane and started the procedure to abandon the plane. I was afraid of the cold if I was taken prisoner, so I wore combat boots, with ram skin. Those boots helped me at that time. I'm not a paratrooper and I confess that when I was to jump I was scared. I tested if I could leave the plane, and put my feet on the stick; I rose the nose of the P-47 and I controlled it. Then my body was left outside the cockpit, but I wasn't over the fuselage, in the right way to abandon the plane. In my fight to control the plane, the Thunderbolt dived, gained speed and to avoid hitting the mountain I pulled the stick and the plane responded to the commands. Then I thought, 'I'm not going to jump.' I lowered my body and sat in the cockpit while they were still firing at me, and I went to the Brenner Pass, flying over Overetto, which was a zone with a lot of flak. I flew very close to a machine-gun position: they hit me and I returned with 57 holes in the fuselage of my plane. When I arrived over Lake Garda, which was on the friendly side [of the front line], I found the helmet, connected the headphones and called Nero. He asked me, 'Where are you? Are you on Rover Jo?' I answered, 'No, I'm flying over Lake Garda, I'm in my plane!' The commander said, 'So you didn't jump?' I explained that I didn't. I found my escadrille and then we returned to our base.

On the sixth mission of the day (number 432), they attacked a big artillery column towed by horses, close to Treviso, destroying it almost completely. On the last sortie of the day, they saw British forces approaching that city.

On 30 April the missions continued, with a total of five, but German resistance in the Po Valley ceased. The Germans only had active troops in the Alps, especially in the area of the Brenner Pass, close to Vittorio Veneto and Treviso, where they were trying to reach

A plane of 2º/9º GAv in 1948, with the A code but without a number. (Author's collection)

The tarmac at Pisa with the planes of the Esquadrilha Verde clearly visible. (Author's collection)

Mechanics repairing a plane. (Author's collection)

German vehicles destroyed during April 1945. (Author's collection)

Meira de Vasconcelos' plane, serialled 44-19662, at Pisa. (Author's collection)

Colonel Nero Moura ready for a mission. (Author's collection)

The end of Desert Lil at Athens. (Author's collection)

Brazilian crews and a US soldier at Landshut airfield in Austria after the war. (Author's collection)

Buyers, Lagares and Pessoa Ramos with the wreck of a Me-262 at Landshut. (John Buyers)

Austria and Germany.

During the spring offensive, the *1º GAvCa* performed 5 percent of all XXII Tactical Air Command missions, but were responsible for destroying 85 percent of the ammunition depots, 36 percent of the fuel depots, 28 percent of the bridges (19 percent of the damaged ones), 15 percent of the motor vehicles (13 percent of the damaged ones) and 10 percent of the animal-towed vehicles (with another 10 percent of the damaged ones). Recalling those says, 2nd Lieutenant Renato Goulart Pereira said:

> Captain Horácio Machado commanded an escadrille where I was No.3 [mission 436]. We went to the north of Italy searching for opportunity targets, because the Germans were performing a disorganized retreat to the north of the Po Valley. We dropped our two bombs on a target we felt was convenient, I believe it was a bridge. Later we continued at very low height to attack vehicles. After some time, and after spending half of our ammunition, the commander decided to return because there were no important targets and fuel was low. When we were climbing at about 1,800ft, I saw a gun towed by six white horses and I asked permission of the commander to descend and attack the formation. However, when I descended and was in shooting range, I was hit by flak. The bullets hit the ammunition box and my bullets began to fire on the left wing. I managed to change course. I had already released the canopy, the seat belt and was at full power, with the plane very hard to control because it was yawing a lot. Immediately my wingman, Lieutenant Lara, put himself below me to accompany me. I managed to gain some altitude and passed Lake Garda. When I was over the lake, Lara told me, 'The fire is reaching the fuselage, you won't manage to hold the plane!' I got scared because I thought I would fall in the mud and I would drown. However, I managed to fly for two or three more minutes and was over land. I stood up, grabbing the windscreen, and the plane launched me over it. I looked down and saw the P-47 falling in a corkscrew. Then I opened the parachute. I touched the ground and when I stood up I saw two British sergeants approaching.

Pereira was the last Brazilian pilot shot down in the war.

The Esquadrilha Azul flightline. (Author's collection)

Standing, from left to right: Aspirante Alberto Bins, First Lieutenant Keller and Aspirante Octavio Moreira Lima. Below: Aspirantes Berthier Figueiredo Prates, Maurício Martins and Fernando Ramos Pereira, at Base Aérea Santa Cruz. (Author's collection)

One of the war veteran P-47s which arrived in Brazil by the end of 1945. (Author's collection)

On 1 May, four sorties took place, all around Udine and Casarsa, in the north-east of Italy. On the first two they performed attacks close to Udine, but on the third, when they reached the city they saw the people waving white flags, indicating the Germans had left, while they watched Allied troops approaching Casarsa. The second mission of the day (number 441) was the last time they used bombs. By the end of the day, the fourth mission only saw Allied troops and partisans occupyng the cities, with no major German presence in the area.

On the following day, 2nd Lieutenant Torres took off for his 100th mission with his escadrille (mission 444), looking for opportunity targets in the Brenner Pass. Torres said:

> The radar controller transmitted solemnly, 'Attention, all flights, do not attack! I repeat, do not attack! War is over!' I felt a chill. I thought of my parents, of the parents of those who were killed. It was an indescribable emotion. It was a mission in which I didn't make any attack, the war was over and the people knew they woud not lose any more comrades.

The last war mission of the *1º GAvCa* happened on that day, when the German forces in Italy, surrounded to the north by Russian and US troops that had already entered Germany and Austria, decided to surrender. This last mission consisted of an armed reconnaissance over the Po Valley performed by Lieutenant Meira de Vasconcelos and Aspirante Roberto Tormin Costa. During the flight they watched the people leaving their houses with white flags when they were told the war was over. Finally, on 8 May, the last German forces surrendered, ending the war in Europe.

After celebrations by the Brazilians in Pisa, on the following day the *1º GAvCa* evaluated their participation in the war. They had used 48 P-47 Thunderbolt, of which 16 were lost in combat and six in accidents. Five pilots were killed in combat and four in accidents, including Gastaldoni in Panama. Eleven pilots jumped safely by parachute and five were made prisoners, returning to the unit after the war. Another seven were moved from the flight because of health problems, so of the 51 original pilots only 24 flew until the end of the war.

12
RETURN WITH GLORY

After the war, the Brazilians remained as an occupation force in Italy until their return was ordered. On 2 June, the pilots began to transfer the 26 Thunderbolts to the depot at Capodichino, where they were prepared for shipping to Brazil. However, on the following day and during these flights, the plane 42-26788 had an accident while landing, suffering serious damage and being written off, although fortunately the pilot was unhurt. The 25 surviving planes of the campaign in Italy were loaded on the UST *W.S. Jennings* cargo ship, together with all the vehicles of the unit and returned to Brazil. The ground personnel embarked on the UST *General M.C. Meigs* on 6 June and departed for home, while the pilots boarded USAAF transport planes and flew to the United States, arriving in New York on 16 June. After they were received by different US authorities, they were given at Kelly Airfield, Texas, a batch of 19 newly built P-47D-30-RAs made to the P-47D-

The reception in the streets of Rio de Janeiro after the war. (Author's collection)

40-RA standard, which had K-1413 sights in place of the Mk-8 used by the Thunderbolts in Italy. They also had S-1 underwing pylons with greater capacity, an AN/APS-13 radar warning system (for the detection of planes behind the P-47, with an amplitude of 60° and 8km range), anti-G flying suits and the capacity for up to five HVAR 127mm rockets under the wings.

On 4 July, they took off, heading to Brazil, on a ferry flight of the new planes, which would replace those Thunderbolts appointed to Brazil in Italy but finally used by US forces. The first stop was at Brownsville, Texas, where they spent the night, and on the following day they continued to Veracruz, Mexico. On 7 July, they flew to San José de Costa Rica, after a stop at Managua, Nicaragua, while on the next day they continued until landing at Albrook Field in the Panama Canal area. On 9 July, they reached Curaçao, in the Dutch Antilles, after a stop at Maracaibo, Venezuela, flying on the 10th to Piarco, Trinidad & Tobago, and on the next day to Macapá in Amapá State, Brazil, after a stop at Paramaribo in Dutch Guiana.

Now in Brazilian territory, on 12 July they continued to Belem and on the next day they stopped at São Luis and Fortaleza until reaching Recife, from where they flew on the 14th to Salvador and on the 15th to Vitória. Finally, on 16 July they reached Campo dos Afonsos in Rio de Janeiro. Before landing, the 19 planes commanded by the war veteran pilots made a low altitude flypast over Rio Branco Avenue in the city centre and continued flying over the coast until reaching Copacabana Fort. Then they went to the aerodrome and 1st Lieutenant Josino Maia de Assis was the first to land because his plane had an oil leak. At Campo dos Afonsos they were received by President Getúlio Vargas, to whom Lieutenant Colonel Nero Moura said: "President, mission accomplished." Some time later, Moura was removed from the Brazilian Air Force and jailed on 29 October for supporting Vargas when a coup d'etat removed him from power.

Two days after the new Thunderbolts arrived home, the ship with the personnel from Italy returned and a flypast was organized with 16 of the new P-47Ds. The reception in Brazil for the veterans lasted many days, with celebrations and parades, but slowly the Second World War veterans returned to their routine, preparing the unit for peacetime at their new base, the Base Aérea Santa Cruz, 25km from Rio de Janeiro.

Appendix I
OPERATIONS OF 1° GAVCA - 31/10/44 TO 03/05/45

Days in operations	184
Missions flown	445
Total combat sorties	2,550
Flying hours in combat missions	5,465
Total flying hours	6,144
Total bombs launched	4,442
Incendiary bombs	166
260lb (125kg) Fragmentation bombs	16
90lb (45kg) Fragmentation bombs	72
1,000lb (500kg) Mk44 Demolition bombs	8
500lb (250kg) Mk43 Demolition bombs	4,180
Approximate tonnage of bombs dropped	1,010
Total ammunition of .50 (12.7mm) calibre used	1,180,200
Total of M8A2 rockets fired	850

Appendix II
RESULTS OBTAINED BY THE 1° GAVCA - 31/10/44 TO 03/05/45

Kind of target	Destroyed	Damaged
Aircraft on the ground	2	9
Locomotives	13	92
Motor transports	1,304	686
Wagons	250	835
Armoured vehicles	8	13
Bridges, railways and roads	25	51
Railways and roads cut	41	-
Railway yards	3	-
Enemy-occupied buildings	144	94
Command posts	2	2
Artillery positions	85	15
Industrial buildings	6	5
Diverse buildings	125	54
Ammunition and fuel depots	31	15
Refineries	3	2
Radar stations	-	2
Boats	19	52
Ships	-	1
Animal-towed vehicles	79	19

Appendix III
REPUBLIC P-47D THUNDERBOLTS USED BY THE FORÇA AÉREA BRASILEIRA IN THE SECOND WORLD WAR

USAF serial	FAB serial	Code	Model	Service entry	Retired	Notes
42-26450	4104	1	P-47D-25RE	28-10-44	17-3-58	Damaged on missions 210 and 434. Assigned to *2ºGC* on 18-7-46. To PqAerAf for repairs on 6-10-48 and used for spares.
42-26753	-	A2	P-47D-25RE	28-10-44	7-11-44	Crashed during a training flight, 2nd Lt. Sapucaia killed.
42-26755	4105	A3	P-47D-25RE	28-10-44	17-3-58	Damaged on missions 260 and 421. Sent to Brazil and assigned to *2ºGC* on 18-7-46. Stored on 10-11-47 until 9-5-55. Retired and scrapped.
42-26756	4106	A4	P-47D-25RE	28-10-44	21-5-46	Damaged on missions183, 254, 328, 367, 417 and 429. Sent to Brazil and assigned to *2ºGC* on 7-1-46. Crashed on 21-5-46 with Lara de Araujo at the commands, who escaped with minor injuries when the plane hit the ground and caught fire.
42-26757	4107	A5	P-47D-25RE	28-10-44	2-12-58	Damaged on missions 275, 346, 381 and 422. Sent to Brazil and assigned to *2ºGC* on 7-1-46. Stored at PqAerAf and later to PqAerSP on 19-10-54. To *1º/4º GAv* on 10-1-57. After its retirement it was used for ground training at Santa Cruz, then as a monument on the base until today.
42-26758	4108	D2	P-47D-25RE	19-11-44	24-10-52	Damaged on missions 215, 249 and 295. Sent to Brazil and assigned to *2ºGC* on 7-1-46. Stored at PqAerAf from 13-4-48 until 30-7-52, when it went to *3º/1º GAvCa*. Crashed on 24-10-52 during a dive bombing practice. 2nd Lt. Dilson Carneiro Dantas killed.
42-26759	-	B1	P-47D-25RE	28-10-44	4-2-45	Shot down during mission 195 over Castel Franco. Pilot Cap. Joel Miranda.
42-26760	4109		P-47D-25RE	28-10-44	14-11-58	Damaged on mission 341. Had an accident at Tarquinia on 21-11-44 and repaired. Sent to Brazil and assigned to *2ºGC* on 7-1-46. Stored at PqAerAf from 5-5-48 and to *2º/9º GAv* on 9-8-51. Stored at PqAerSP on 21-1-54. To *1º/4º GAv* on 8-8-57. After its retirement was used for ground training. On 30-12-68 sent to the *Museu de Aeronáutica da Fundação Santos Dumont São Paulo*. Later to the *Museu Asas de um Sonho* of TAM airline in São Paulo until today
42-26761	-	C6	P-47D-25RE	28-10-44	7-2-45	Crashed while taking off at Pisa. Pilot Aspirante Fernandio Pereyron Mocellin unhurt.
42-26762	4110	C1	P-47D-25RE	19-1-45	30-12-52	Damaged on mission 298. Sent to Brazil and assigned to *2ºGC* on 7-1-46. Stored at PqAerAf on 12-5-48. Used for ground training from 30-12-52. Now used as a monment at *Casa do Expedicionario*, Curitiba
42-26763	-	B3	P-47D-25RE	28-10-44	6-11-44	Shot down on 15-2-45 during mission 222.
42-26764	-	D1	P-47D-25RE	28-10-44	21-4-45	Damaged on missions 180, 248 and 332. Crashed at Pisa with Capt. Pessoa Ramos, who escaped.
42-26766	-	B4	P-47D-25RE	28-10-44	26-3-45	Shot down by the flak. Pilot 1st Lt. Correa Neto unhurt.
42-26768	-	B5	P-47D-25RE	28-10-44	2-1-45	Had an accident on 26-11-44 and repaired. Shot down, pilot 2nd Lt. Campos de Medeiros killed.
42-26772	4111	B1	P-47D-25RE	2-1-45	17-3-58	Damaged on missions 255, 383, 386 and 429. Sent to Brazil and assigned to *2ºGC* on 7-1-46. Stored at PqAerSP on 9-5-55 until it was scrapped.
42-26773	-	D6	P-47D-25RE	28-10-44	22-4-45	Damaged on missions 248 and 341. Shot down on mission 381. Pilot 2nd Lt. Coelho de Magalhaes unhurt.
42-26774	-	D3	P-47D-27RE	28-10-44	17-2-45	Minor accident on 30-11-44 at Tarquinia. Crashed at Pisa. Pilot Aspirante João Milton Prates unhurt.
42-26775	-	B6	P-47D-27RE	19-11-44	10-2-45	Damaged on mission 187. Shot down on 10-2-45. Pilot 1st Lt. Brandini injured and captured.
42-26776	-	A2	P-47D-27RE	28-10-44	7-3-45	Damaged on missions 189 and 217. Shot down on 7-3-45. Pilot Captain Kopp escaped unhurt.
42-26778	4112	C2	P-47D-27RE	28-10-44	4-11-49	Damaged on missions 298, 335, 394 and 440. Sent to Brazil and assigned to *2ºGC* on 7-1-46. Crashed at Santa Cruz.

USAF serial	FAB serial	Code	Model	Service entry	Retired	Notes
42-26779	4113	C3	P-47D-27RE	28-10-44	19-7-57	Damaged on missions 205, 334, 420 and 429. Sent to Brazil and assigned to *2ºGC* on 7-1-46. Stored at PqAerAf on 5-5-48. To *2º/1º GAv* on 30-7-52. To *3º/1º GAvCa*. Stored at PqAerSP on 5-1-54 and later to *2º/5º GAv* until 1-1-57 when was sent to *1º/4º GAv*. Lost in an accident.
42-26780	4115	C4	P-47D-27RE	28-10-44	2-12-58	Damaged on missions 389, 403 and 413. Sent to Brazil and assigned to *2ºGC* on 7-1-46. Stored at PqAerAf on 13-4-48. To *3º/1º GAv* on 27-11-52 and on 28-12-53 sent to PqAerSP for storage. To *1º/4º GAv* on 10-1-57 until its retirement. Scrapped.
42-26782	-		P-47D-27RE	28-10-44	6-11-44	Shot down on mission 20. Pilot 2nd Lt. Cordeiro e Silva killed.
42-26783	-	2	P-47D-27RE	28-10-44	4-2-45	Minor accident at Tarquinia on 19-11-44. Repaired. Shot down on mission 199. Pilot 2nd Lt. Moura unhurt.
42-26784	-	A1	P-47D-27RE	28-10-44	9-4-45	Damaged on mission 212. Shot down on mission 324. Pilot 2nd Lt. Souza Coelho escaped unhurt.
42-26786	4114	D4	P-47D-27RE	28-10-44	2-12-58	Damaged on missions 268, 389 and 430. Sent to Brazil and assigned to *2ºGC* on 7-1-46. To *1º/4º GAv* on 10-1-57. Lost in an accident on 17-12-57 while being ferried to PqAerSP.
42-26788	-	A2	P-47D-27RE	28-10-44	3-6-45	Damaged on missions 215, 267, 297, 334, 368 and 386. Crashed while landing at Capodichino on 3-6-45.
42-28986	4116	B6	P-47D-28RA	19-1-45	17-3-58	Damaged on missions 204, 240 and 372. Sent to Brazil and assigned to *2ºGC* on 7-1-46. Minor accident on 22-10-52 at Santa Cruz. On 15-7-53 sent for repairs to PqAerAf and later to PqAerSP, where it was used for spares and scrapped.
42-29265	4117		P-47D-28RA	12-2-45	17-3-58	Sent to Brazil and assigned to *2ºGC* on 7-1-46. Stored at PqAerAf on 10-11-47 and later to PqAerSP, where it was used for spares and scrapped.
44-19659	-	C6	P-47D-28RE	28-10-44	16-11-44	Lost over Tarquinia when collided with a USAAF C-47 during the filming of a documentary.
44-19660	4118	C5	P-47D-28RE	28-10-44	27-6-46	Damaged on mission 396. Sent to Brazil and assigned to *2ºGC* on 7-1-46. Crashed at Baia de Sepetiba.
44-19661	-	D2	P-47D-28RE	28-10-44	29-1-45	Shot down on mission 188. Pilot 1st Lt. Josino Maia de Assis captured.
44-19662	4119	D5	P-47D-28RE	28-10-44	17-3-58	Damaged on missions 242, 263, 318, 358 and 414. Sent to Brazil and assigned to *2ºGC* on 7-1-46. Stored at PqAerAf on 1-10-48 and later to PqArSP, for use as spares and scrapped.
44-19663	4120	A6	P-47D-28RE	28-10-44	17-9-53	Lost part of its right wing on mission 184. Damaged on missions 209, 244 and 341. Sent to Brazil and assigned to *2ºGC* on 7-1-46. Stored at PqAerAf on 10-11-47. To *2º/9º GAv* on 22-7-49. Minor accident on 12-5-52 at Santa Cruz, other accidents on 30-4-53 and 14-7-53. Stored at PqAerSP on 17-9-53. On 15-4-59 started to be used for ground training. Installed as monument at the *Escola de Ensinos Aeronáuticos* in 1968. Preserved at the *Museu Aeroespacial* at Río de Janeiro.
44-19665	-	A6	P-47D-28RE	28-10-44	23-12-44	Minor accident on 20-11-44 at Maglione Field at Siena. Shot down during mission 107 close to Quistello. Pilot 1st Lt. Ismael de Motta Paes captured.
44-19666	-	B6	P-47D-28RE	12-2-45	22-1-45	Shot down on mission 178 close to Milan. Pilot 1st Lt. Aurélio Vieira Sampaio killed.
44-19667	-	B2	P-47D-28RE	28-10-44	7-1-45	Crashed during a training flight on 7-1-45 at Lago Massacuaccoli. Pilot Aspirante Av. Frederico Gustavo dos Santos unhurt.
44-20338	-	C6	P-47D-30RE	28-10-44	30-4-45	Damaged on mission 272. Shot down to the north of Venice during mission 436. Pilot 2nd Lt. Renato Goulart Pereira unhurt.
44-20339	-	D3	P-47D-30RE	20-2-45	13-4-45	Lost during mission 331 close to Spilimbergo when the fuel depots it was attacking exploded. Pilot Aspirante Av. Frederico Gustavo dos Santos killed.
44-20345	4121	D3	P-47D-30RE	1945	2-7-48	Damaged on missions 259, 304 and 395. Sent to Brazil and assigned to *2ºGC* on 7-1-46. Lost in an accident.

USAF serial	FAB serial	Code	Model	Service entry	Retired	Notes
44-20800	4122	B4	P-47D-30RE	1945	15-4-52	Damaged on missions 346 and 435. Sent to Brazil and assigned to *2ºGC* on 7-1-46. Had a mid-air collision with 4163, 2nd Lt. J.S. Porto killed.
44-20850	4123	D1	P-47D-30RE	1945	1953	Damaged on missions 341, 366 and 417. Sent to Brazil and assigned to *2ºGC* on 7-1-46. Transferred to PqAerSP on 28-12-53 where it was used for spares and scrapped.
44-20854	4124	A1	P-47D-30RE	1945	27-7-48	Damaged on missions 346, 351, 368, 387, 422 and 429. Sent to Brazil and assigned to *2ºGC* on 7-1-46. Used for spares.
44-21022	-	2	P-47D-30RE	1945	26-4-45	Shot down on mission 413 over Alessandria, pilot 1st Lt. Luiz Lopes Dornelles killed.
44-21093	4125	2	P-47D-30RE	1945	29-2-53	Sent to Brazil and assigned to *2ºGC* on 7-1-46. Used for spares.
44-33090	4126		P-47D-30RA	1945	1-9-48	Sent to Brazil and assigned to *2ºGC* on 7-1-46. Used for spares.
44-33093	4127	B3	P-47D-30RE	1945	24-1-49	Damaged on mission 258. Sent to Brazil and assigned to *2ºGC* on 7-1-46. Crashed at Petrópolis, 2nd Lt. Raymundo Silvares de Barreiras killed.
44-33097	4128		P-47D-30RA	1945	1953	Damaged on mission 414. Sent to Brazil, had an accident during a test flight on 13-12-45, assigned to *2ºGC* on 7-1-46 but only used for ground training. Later scrapped.
The following planes were assigned to the *1ºGAvCa* during the war but were later delivered to USAAF units: 42-26754, 42-26765, 42-26767, 42-26769, 42-26770, 42-26771, 42-26777, 42-26781, 42-26785, 42-26787, 42-26789, 44-19664, 44-19668, 44-20340, 44-20341, 44-20342, 44-20343, 44-20344, 44-20346, 44-20347, 44-20799, 44-20802, 44-20803, 44-20804, 44-20805 and 44-20806.						

Appendix IV
GERMAN AND ITALIAN SUBMARINES THAT OPERATED IN THE SOUTH ATLANTIC

Alpino Bagnolini, Liuzzi class, commissioned in 1938, operated off Brazil between March and April 1942. No ships sunk in the area. Transferred to the German *Kriegsmarine* in 1943 for use as a transport submarine under the name *Aquila II*, then *Mercator II* and later *UIT-22*. Sunk on 11 March 1943 off the South African coast, while en route to Japan.

Archimede, Brin class, commissioned in 1939, operated off Brazil between May and June 1942. On 15 June sank the Panamanian Freighter *Cardina*. On 24 February 1943 departed again for Brazil, but on 15 April was sunk by three US Navy Catalinas of VP-83. Only one survivor.

Barbarigo, Marcello class, commissioned in 1938, operated off Brazil between April and May 1942. On 18 May damaged the Brazilian freighter *Comandante Lyra*. While returning from patrol she sank the British merchant ship *Chalbury*. Lost without a trace in June 1943 when travelling with cargo to Japan.

Comandante Alfredo Cappellini, Marcello class, commissioned in 1940, operated off Brazil in May 1942. No ships sunk in the area. Transferred to the German *Kriegsmarine* in 1943 for use as a transport submarine under the name *Aquila III*, later *UIT-24*. When Germany surrendered was taken by the Japanese Navy as *I-503*, captured by the US forces and sank off Kobe on 16 April 1946.

Enrico Tazzoli, Calvi class, commissioned in 1936, operated off Brazil between December 1942 and February 1943. On 12 December sank the British ship *Empire Hawk* and the Dutch ship *Ombilin*. On 21 December sunk the British ship *Queen City* and on the 25 sank the US ship *Doña Aurora*. After returning to Bordeaux, she was modified into a transport vessel, but lost between 18 and 24 May for unknown reasons on her voyage to Japan. No survivors.

Leonardo da Vinci, Marconi class, commissioned in 1940, in early 1942 operated near the US coast, where she sank the *Cabedello* on 25 February, with no survivors. Operated between Natal and Bahía on May without success, before going in June to the African coast. Destroyed on 23 May 1943 by the British destroyer HMS *Active* and frigate HMS *Ness*.

Luigi Torelli, Marconi class, commissioned in 1940. Arrived off the Brazilian coast in March 1943 and on the 16th was attacked by airplanes, receiving heavy damage and one killed, forcing the vessel to return to its base. After that, she was transformed into a transport and transferred to the German *Kriegsmarine* as *UIT-25* until taken over by the Japanese on 10 May 1945, being renamed *I-504*. Scuttled by the US Navy after the Japanese surrender.

Pietro Calvi, Calvi class, commissioned in 1936. Arrived off the Brazilian coast on March 1942, on the 29th attacked and sank the British freighter *Tredinnick* and on the 31st spotted the US tanker *T.C. McCobb* which was sunk on the following day, being the first American ship sunk by an Italian submarine. On 9 April the submarine sank the American tanker *Eugene V.R. Thayer*, followed later by the Norwegian ship *Balkis* and the Panamanian tanker *Ben Brush*. After that, it returned to base. Sunk on 13 July 1942 by British sloop HMS *Lulworth*.

U-128, Type IXC, commissioned on 12 May 1941, operated off Brazil between May 1942 and July 1942, sinking the US freighter *Steel Engineer*. Returned to Brazilian waters between November 1942 and January 1943, but no sinkings. Back to Brazil in May 1943, located by Mariner serialled P-2 of VP-74 on 16 May south of Pernambuco and attacked unsuccessfully, found again by Mariners P-5 and P-6 of the same unit on the following day, which damaged her, making it impossible to dive. Then intercepted by US destroyers USS *Moffett* and USS *Jouett*. Abandoned and sunk with gun fire. Seven dead, 47 survivors.

U-154, Type IXC, commissioned on 2 August 1941, went to operate off Brazil on May 1943, on the 8th attacked the *Motocarline* unsuccessfully. On 27th attacked convoy BT-14 and sank the freighter *John Worthington*, damaged the *Cardinal Gibbons* and the tanker *Florida*. Returned to France in July and back to Brazil between October and December 1943. Sunk on 3 July 1944 near Madeira Islands by US destroyers.

U-161, Type IXC, commissioned on 8 July 1941, operated off Brazil between May and June 1942, with no sinkings in the area. Operated unsuccessfully close to Brazil again in November and December 1942. Returned to Brazil in September 1943; on the 26th sank the Brazilian freighter *Itapagé*, then located by a Mariner of VP-74 but escaped the attack. On the following day was located by another Mariner of the unit, serialled P-2, piloted by Lt. Patterson, who dropped six depth charges and strafed the submarine, but the damage received from the *U-161*'s guns forced the plane to return to base. A Lockheed Ventura of the US Navy arrived later but no trace of the submarine was ever found.

U-164, Type IXC, commissioned on 28 November 1941, arrived off the Brazilian coast in November 1942. On 1 January 1943 sank the *Brageland*, and on 6 January attacked by the Catalina serialled P-2, piloted by Lt. Ford of VP-83, off Pernambuco. Four depth charges dropped, which split the submarine into two, with only two survivors.

U-170, Type IXC, commissioned on 19 January 1943, arrived off Brazil in September 1943. On 23 October sank the Brazilian freighter *Campos*, then left in November. Surrendered on 9 May 1945, sunk by the British on 30 November 1945.

U-177, Type IXD, commissioned on 14 March 1942, operated in the South Atlantic and sunk on 6 February 1944 1,000km to the south-west of Ascension Island by depth charges from a US Liberator aircraft serialled B-3 of VB-107 Squadron. Ten survivors, 50 killed.

U-180, Type IXD, commissioned on 16 May 1942. Returning from a trip to the Far East on 3 June 1943, sank the freighter *Boris* to the north-west of Ascension Island. Disappeared in August 1944.

U-182, Type IXD, commissioned on 30 June 1942. Returning from the Indian Ocean, on 1 May 1943 sank the Greek freighter *Adelfotis* 1,000km north-west of Ascension Island. Sunk by destroyer USS *Mackenzie* on 16 May.

U-185, Type IXC, commissioned on 13 June 1942. Arrived off the coast of Brazil in July 1943, and on the 7th attacked convoy BT18, 150 miles north-east of Natal, sinking the US tanker *William Boyce Thompson*, the US freighter *James Robertson* and the *Thomas Sinnickson*, while damaging the tanker *S.B. Hunt*. On 1 August sank the Brazilian freighter *Bagé*, which was lagging behind convoy TJ2. On 6 August sank the Brazilian freighter *Fort Halkett* to the south of Recife. On 11 August rendezvoused with the *U-604*, which was seriously damaged, and the *U-172*, to rescue the crew of *U-604* and sink the vessel. When they were doing so they were found by a Liberator of VP-107 piloted by Lt. Cdr. Prueber, who attacked the submarines. The *U-172* dived and the *U-185* shot down the bomber on its third attack. After sinking the *U-604*, on the night of 14 August they transferred part of their crew to the *U-172*. After starting their return, on 24 November they were found by a Grumman Wildcat from the aircraft carrier USS *Core*, and attacked by them and a Grumman Avenger, who sunk the submarine - 39 of the crew survived.

U-199, Type IXD, commissioned on 28 November 1942 and arrived off Brazil in May 1943. On 22 June sank the small Brazilian sail vessel *Shangri-La*, and on the 24th the British freighter *Henzada*, also attacking the US freighter *Charles Wilson Peale* on 27 June without success. Attacked by a US Navy Mariner of VP-74 on 3 July, but the plane crashed. *U-199* was sunk on the following day by a Mariner of VP-74, a Brazilian Hudson and a Catalina, with 12 survivors and 50 killed.

U-460, Type XIV, commissioned on 24 December 1941. Operated in the central Atlantic resupplying other U-Boats until being sunk on 4 October 1943 by Grumman Avengers to the north of the Azores.

U-466, Type VIIC, commissioned on 17 June 1942. Arrived near French Guiana in June 1943 and operated in the area until August without sinking ships. Damaged by an air raid on Toulon on 5 July 1944 and later sunk.

U-507, Type IXC, commissioned on 8 October 1941 and arrived off the Brazilian coast in July 1942. On the 16th sank the Brazilian freighters *Baependy*, *Araraquara* and *Annibal Benévolo* to the south of Aracajú. On the following day sank the *Itagiba* and *Arará* near Salvador, on the 19th the *Jacyra* sail ship and on the 22nd the Swedish merchant ship *Hammaren*. Their actions against Brazilian ships led to the declaration of war by the country on the Axis powers. Left for the African coast in August and returned in December. On the 27th sunk the British freighter *Oakbank* and on 3 January 1943 the British ship *Baron Dechmont*, while on the 8th sank the British ship *Yorkwood*. On 13 January, she was spotted near Natal by the Catalina serialled P-10 of VP-83, piloted by Lt. Ludwig, who sank her with depth charges. All 55 on board were killed.

U-510, Type IXC, commissioned on 25 November 1941. Approached the area of the Guianas in March 1943, sinking on the night of the 8th the British ship *Kelvinbank* and the US freighter *James K. Polk*, and damaged the US freighters *George G. Meade*, *Tabitha Brown*, *Joseph Rodman Drake*, *Mark Hanna*, *James Smith* and *Thomas Ruffin*. After that returned to France, and in June returned to the coast of French Guiana, sinking on 8 July the *B.P. Newton*, a Norwegian tanker, and the US freighter *Eldena*, and damaging the *Everagra* freighter off Letonia. Two days later captured and sank the Swedish freighter *Scandinavia* and later returned to France. On 9 May 1945 surrendered in France; pressed into service by the French Navy as *Bouan*, retired in 1959 and scrapped in 1960.

U-513, Type IXC, commissioned on 10 January 1942. Arrived off the Brazilian coast in May 1943, and on 21 June sank the Swedish freighter *Venezia* near Rio de Janeiro, then on the 25th damaged the US freighter *Eagle*. On 1 July sank the Brazilian ship *Tutóia* and two days later the US freighter *Elihu B. Wassburne*, and on the 16th the Richard Caswell. On 19 July spotted near Florianópolis by the Martin Mariner serialled P-5 of VP-74, commanded by Lt. Whitcomb, who dropped depth charges and made two hits, sinking the vessel. Seven survivors and 46 dead.

U-515, Type IXC, commissioned on 21 February 1942, operated between Trinidad and Brazil between August and October 1942. Sunk on 9 April 1944 by the destroyer USS *Chatelain* and airplanes; 16 killed and 44 survivors.

U-518, Type IXC, commissioned on 25 April 1942. Arrived off Brazil in January 1943. On 18 February sank the Brazilian freighter *Brasiloide* near Bahía and on the 28th detected convoy BT6, sinking on the following day the US merchantman *Fritz-John Porter*. On 20 March sank the Dutch ship *Marisso* and on the 25th the Swedish *Industria*, returning to France after that. Sunk on 22 April 1945 by destroyers USS *Carter* and *Neal A. Scott*. No survivors among the 57 crew members.

U-590, Type VIIC, commissioned on 2 October 1941. Arrived off the Brazilian coast in June 1943, and on 4 July sank the Brazilian freighter *Pelotaslóide* near Marajó Bay. On 9 July spotted by a Catalina of VP-94, piloted by Lt. Hare, near Maracá Island in the Amazon River mouth. During the attack, the pilot and radio-operator of the plane were killed by gunfire from *U-590*, with the co-pilot taking the controls and attempting a second unsuccessful attack before returning to base. Two hours later it was attacked by the Catalina serialled P-1 of the same unit, with pilot Lt. Auslander, who dropped six depth charges and destroyed the submarine, with 45 killed and no survivors.

U-591, Type VIIC, commissioned on 9 October 1941, and arrived off Brazil in July 1943. On 30 July was located near Natal by the Ventura serialled B-6 of VB-127, commanded by Lt. Young, and sunk with depth charges: 19 killed and 28 survivors.

U-598, Type VIIC, commissioned on 27 November 1941 and arrived off Brazil in July 1943. Spotted on 22 July by the Liberator piloted by Lt. Cdr. Turner of VB-107, near Natal, forcing her to dive. Another plane joined the action but the submarine was lost. On the following day she was found again and damaged, impeding her ability to dive. A Liberator piloted by Lt. Waugh made an attack, but was destroyed by the debris from the explosions of its own charges, as they were flying too low. Shortly after the plane serialled B-6, with Lt. Ford at the controls, hit the submarine, which sank with just two survivors and 44 dead.

U-604, Type VIIC, commissioned on 8 February 1942. Arrived off the Brazilian coast in July 1943 and found on 30 July by a Lockheed Ventura of VB-129, commanded by Lt. Cdr. Davies, 100 miles off Maceió. The submarine dived when the plane dropped four Mk-47 depth charges, but was seriously damaged and could not return to its base. On 3 August it was unsuccessfully attacked by a Liberator of VB-107. Despite a planned rendezvous with *U-185* to transfer the crew and then sink the *U-604* on 8 August, intense air activity forced a delay until the 11th, when they were also joined by the *U-172*. They were found by another Liberator of VB-107, piloted by Lt. Cdr. Prueher. The *U-172* dived and the other two repelled the attack, destroying the plane. After transferring the crew to the *U-185*, the *U-604* was sunk. Fourteen crew members had died during the actions and 31 survived.

U-653, Type VIIC, commissioned on 25 May 1941. Operated shortly and without success to the north of the Amazon River mouth between July and August 1943. Sunk on 15 March 1944 by HMS *Starling*, with no survivors.

U-662, Type VIIC, commissioned on 9 April 1942. Approached the area between Trinidad and the Amazon River mouth in July 1943. On the 19th found by a USAAF Liberator operating from Surinam, and on the 20th attacked by a USAAF B-18 Bolo near Cayenne. On the following day she was found by two US Navy Catalinas near Cassiporé Cape in Brazilian waters, and sunk by the plane commanded by Lt. Howland. There were just two survivors and 46 killed.

U-848, Type IXD, commissioned on 20 February 1943. Arrived in the South Atlantic in November 1943 and detected on the 5th to the south-west of Ascension Island. Attacked unsuccessfully by three Liberators of VB-107, one of which returned damaged. Later, two B-25 Mitchells of the 1st Compron (Composite Squadron) of the USAAF bombed the submarine but scored no hits, but this attack was followed by another two Liberators with depth charges, who sank the submarine. All 64 of the crew were killed.

U-861, Type IXD, commissioned on 2 June 1943. Arrived in May 1944 off the Brazilian coasts to attack the *William Mann* transport, which was carrying the first troops of the FEB, but never found the ship. On 20 July it sank the Brazilian Navy transport *Vital d'Oliveira* to the east of Rio de Janeiro and attacked unsuccessfully the submarine hunter *Javari*. On the 24th attacked convoy JT39 and sank the US freighter *William Gaston*. After that, she left for the African coast. Surrendered on 9 May 1945 and sunk by gunfire from the Polish destroyer *Blyskawica* on 8 December 1945.

U-863, Type IXD, commissioned on 3 November 1943. On its first patrol she was detected off the coast of Recife on 29 September 1944 by a Liberator of VB-107, piloted by Lt. Burton, operating from Natal. After being damaged by depth charges in a first attack, the plane made a second pass, firing its machine guns, as the release mechanism of the remaining charges failed. A second Liberator, serialled B-9 and piloted by Lt. Krug, arrived and attacked the submarine with depth charges, while both planes also strafed her with their machine guns. The crew started to abandon the vessel when she was hit again by depth charges. A third Liberator arrived when the action was ending and dropped life rafts for about 20 survivors seen on the water, but they were never recovered. All 68 crew died.

Appendix V
BRAZILIAN SHIPS LOST

Buarque, sunk on 16 February 1942 60 miles off Hatteras Cape, North Carolina, by *U-432*. One killed, 84 rescued.

Olinda, sunk on 18 February 1942 by the guns of *U-432* near Virginia, USA. 46 survivors.

Cabedelo, sunk with all hands by *Leonardo da Vinci* on 25 February 1942 near Philadelphia.

Arabutã, sunk near Hatteras Cape on 7 March 1942 by *U-155*. One killed, 50 survivors.

Cayrú, sunk by *U-94* on 8 March 1942, 130 nautical miles from New York. 53 killed, 36 survivors.

Parnaíba, sunk by *U-162* near Barbados on 1 May 1942. Seven killed, 65 survivors.

Commandante Lyra, sunk by the *Barbarigo* near Fernando de Noronha on 18 May 1942. Two killed, 50 survivors.

Gonçalves Dias, destroyed by *U-502* near Key West on 24 May 1942. Six killed, 46 survivors.

Alegrete, sunk by *U-156* near Santa Lucía on 1 June 1942. 64 survivors.

Vidal de Negreiros, sunk by *U-156* together with *Alegrete*.

Paracuri, attacked on 5 June 1942 by U-159 in the North Atlantic.

Pedrinhas, torpedoed by *U-203* near Puerto Rico on 26 June 1942. 48 survivors.

Tamandaré, sunk by *U-66* near Port of Spain on 26 June 1942. Four killed and 48 survivors.

Barbacena, destroyed by *U-66* near Tobago on 24 July 1942. Six killed, 56 survivors.

Piave, sunk near Tobago by *U-155* on 28 July 1942. One killed, 34 survivors.

Baependi, torpedoed by *U-507* on 15 August 1942 along the Brazilian north-east coast. 270 killed and 36 survivors. First of a series of six attacks that led to the Brazilian declaration of war.

Aníbal Benévolo, sunk by *U-507* on 16 August 1942 at Sergipe. 130 killed and four survivors.

Araraquara, destroyed by *U-507* on 17 August 1942 at Sergipe. 131 killed and 11 survivors.

Itagiba, sunk by *U-507* on 17 August 1942 near Bahía. 39 killed and 145 survivors.

Arará, destroyed by *U-507* when rescuing the survivors of *Itagiba* on 17 August. 32 dead and 15 survivors.

Jacira, last victim of the *U-507* in its raid, on 19 August 1942, in the area of Bahía. Six survivors.

Osório, sunk near the coast of Pará by *U-514* on 27 September 1942. Five killed and 34 survivors.

Lajes, sunk together with the *Osório* by the same submarine. Three killed and 46 survivors.

Antonico, destroyed close to French Guiana by *U-516* on 28 September 1942. 16 killed, 24 survivors.

Porto Alegre, sunk near Durban, South Africa, by U-504 on 3 November 1942. One killed and 40 survivors.

Apaloide, sunk by *U-163* on 22 November 1942 close to Venezuela. Three killed and 53 survivors.

Brasiloide, destroyed by *U-518* on 18 February 1943 near Sergipe. 50 survivors.

Afonso Pena, destroyed on 2 March 1943 by the *Barbarigo* near Bahía. 125 killed, 117 survivors.

Tutoia, sunk by *U-513* near São Paulo on 31 June 1943. Seven killed and 30 survivors.

Pelotasloide, sunk near Pará River mouth by *U-590* on 4 July 1943. Five killed and 37 survivors.

Shangri-La, destroyed by *U-199* on 22 July 1943 at Arraial do Cabo. 10 killed, no survivors.

Bagé, sunk by *U-185* at Sergipe on 31 July 1943. 26 killed, 106 survivors.

Itapagé, destroyed near Alagoas on 26 September 1943 by *U-161*. 22 killed and 84 survivors.

Cisne Branco, sunk after a collision on 27 September 1943, possibly by enemy action, near Canoa Quebrada, Ceará. Four killed and six survivors.

Campos, sunk on 23 October 1943 by *U-170* near the coast of São Paulo state. 12 and 51 survivors.

Vital de Oliveira, destroyed on 19 July 1944 by *U-861* near Farol de São Tomé, Rio de Janeiro. 99 killed and 176 survivors.

Appendix VI
RANKS

- *Ten Cel*: *Tenente Coronel*, Lieutenant Colonel.
- *Maj-Av*: *Major-Aviador*, Major-Aviator.
- *Cap-Av*: *Capitão-Aviador*, Captain-Aviator.
- *1º* and *2º Ten-Av*: *Tenente-Aviador*, 1st and 2nd Lieutenant-Aviator.
- *Asp.-Av. da res. Conv*: *Aspirante da Aviação da Reserva Convocado*, Aspirant from the reserve called up for duty.

BIBLIOGRAPHY

Aparecido Camazano Alamino, *Bombardeiros bimotores da FAB* (São Paulo: C&R Editorial, 2008).

João Barone, *1942, o Brasil e sua guerra quase desconhecida* (Rio de Janeiro: Nova Fronteira Participações, 2013).

Mauro Lins de Barros, *P-47 Thunderbolt in Brasil, 1945-1957* (Brazil: Adler Editora, 2005).

Jackson Flores Jr., *Aeronaves Militares Brasileiras 1916-2015* (Rio de Janeiro: Action Editora, 2016).

Durval de Noronha Goyos Jr., *A campanha da Força Expedicionária Brasileira pela libertação da Itália* (São Paulo: Cultura Académica Editora, 2013).

Dan Hagedorn, *Conquistadors of the Sky. A History of Aviation in Latin America* (Florida: Univeristy Press of Florida, 2008).

John R. Harrison, *Fairwing Brazil: Tales of the South Atlantic in World War II* (Atglen PA: Schiffer Books, 2014).

Instituto Histórico Cultural da Aeronáutica, *Historia Geral da Aeronáutica Brasileira, Volume 3* (Brazil: 1991).

Lieutenant-Brigadier Nelson Freire Lavenere-Wanderley, *Historia da Força Aérea Brasileira* (Brazil: Ministerio da Aeronáutica, 1975).

Lieutenant-Brigadier Nelson Freire Lavenere-Wanderley, *La Fuerza Aérea Brasileña durante la II Guerra Mundial* (Brazil: Ministerio de Aeronáutica).

Brigadier Rui Moreira Lima, *Senta a Pua!* (Belo Horizonte, ed., Itatiaia, 1980).

Rui Moreira Lima y José Rebelo Meira de Vasconcelos, *Heróis dos Céus* (Rio de Janeiro: Action Editora, 2004).

Francisco Pereira Netto, *Aviação Militar Brasileira, 1916-1984* (Rio de Janeiro: Revista Aeronáutica Editora, 1984).

Magazines

'O vôo do Arará', *Força Aérea*, No.1.

'O Trator Voador', Jackson Flores Jr, *Força Aérea*, No.5.

'Thunderbolt, o destruidor', Claudio Lucchesi, *Asas*, No.1.

'Douglas A-20 Havoc, o devastador da FAB', Claudio Lucchesi, *Asas*, No.6.

'Vultee V-11GB, nosso bombardeio de ataque', José Ribeiro de Mendonça and Claudio Lucchesi, *Asas*, No.9.

'B-25 Mitchell, Uma lenda nas cores da FAB', Paulo Kasseb, *Asas*, No.21.

'O Brasil na batalha do Atlántico', Claudio Lucchesi, *Asas*, No.25.

'Aviação Naval da Marinha, as asas pioneiras', Claudio Lucchesi, *Asas*, No.28.

'Douglas A-20K Havoc na FAB', Aparecido Camazano Alamino, *Asas*, No.36.

'B-25 na FAB', Aparecido Camazano Alamino, *Asas*, No.40.

'Curtiss P-40, um caça puro-sangue na FAB', Aparecido Camazano Alamino, *Asas*, No.40.

'Lockheed-Vega B-34 Ventura na FAB', Aparecido Camazano Alamino, *Asas*, No.44.

'Consolidated PBY-5 Catalina na FAB', Aparecido Camazano Alamino, *Asas*, No.45.

'Focke Wulf Fw-58 *Weihe* no Brasil', Aparecido Camazano Alamino, *Asas*, No.46.

'Curtiss P-36A na FAB', Aparecido Camazano Alamino, *Asas*, No.47.

'Vultee V-11 no Brasil', Aparecido Camazano Alamino, *Asas*, No.51.

'Douglas C-47 na FAB', Aparecido Camazano Alamino, *Asas*, No.52.

'Os 33 do Pacífico', Paulo Bastos, Hélio Higuchi and Ricardo Lavecchia, *Tecnología & Defesa*, No.138.

'Fantasmas galopantes da costa brasileira', Alan C. Carey, *Força Aérea*, Nos.91 and 92.

Websites

Associação Brasileira de Pilotos de Caça: www.abra-pc.com.br

Historia de la Fuerza Aérea Brasileña, by Rudnei Dias da Cunha: www.rudnei.cunha.com.br

1º GAvCa in Italia: www.jambock.com.br

Sentando a Pua!: www.sentandoapua.com.br

Regia Marina: www.regiamarina.net

U-Historia: www.u-historia.com

ABOUT THE AUTHOR

Santiago Rivas was born in Buenos Aires, Argentina in 1977. Twenty years later, the Journalism graduate started to work in the fields of aviation and defence journalism – travelling all across Latin America to conduct his research for articles and books.

In 2007 he published his first book, which was about the Malvinas/Falklands War, for a Brazilian editor – and since then another 12 have been published across the globe in Argentina, Brazil, France, Germany and the United Kingdom, while four more are soon to be released. He has also had articles published in more than 50 magazines in 20 countries – and he currently works for more than 20 of the magazines.

Santiago has three children and lives in Buenos Aires. He continues to travel every year to most of the Latin American countries to fulfil his research-based work.